CRACKER

The Cracker Culture in Florida History

Dana Ste.Claire

D1510616

UNIVERSITY PRESS OF FLORIDA

Gainesville/Tallahassee/Tampa/Boca Raton
Pensacola/Orlando/Miami/Jacksonville/Ft. Myers/Sarasota

21 20 19 18 17   8 7 6 5 4

Library of Congress Catalog Card Number: 97-074499
ISBN 978-0-8130-3028-9

The University Press of Florida is the scholarly publishing agency for the State
University System of Florida, comprising Florida A & M University, Florida Atlantic
University, Florida Gulf Coast University, Florida International University, Florida
State University, New College of Florida, University of Central Florida, University of
Florida, University of North Florida, University of South Florida, and University of
West Florida.

University Press of Florida
15 Northwest 15th Street
Gainesville, FL 32611-2079
http://upress.ufl.edu

Cracker has been financed in part with grant assistance provided by
the Museum of Florida History
Bureau of Historical Museums
Division of Historical Resources, Florida Department of State.
A Florida Heritage book

Cover: Image adapted from "A Pair of Georgia Crackers," from *The Great South*
by Edward King, 1875, p. 372.

Dedicated to
Jim Bob and Dottie Tinsley,
longtime family friends.
Life is a wonderful circle, indeed.

And to
Dave and Gloria Burnell
true Florida Crackers,
and true Cracker friends.

Contents

Foreword

by James M. Denham

This volume – part anthology, part anthropology, part history, part folklore – celebrates Florida's rich and diverse Cracker heritage. Dana Ste.Claire and The Museum of Arts and Sciences in Daytona Beach deserve much praise for bringing together these vivid images of Florida's frontier people who did not just live but *flourished* in a time before air conditioning, mosquito repellant, and screens. While many of these depictions of Crackers may seem negative or ambivalent to modern tastes, Ste.Claire's work reminds us that "Cracker Culture" and ways also offer positive legacies valuable for our present generation: self-reliance, self-sufficiency, honesty, and finally a simple, direct approach to people and problems. These are only a few of the traits passed down through the generations.

Despised, caricatured, misunderstood, and patronized, Florida's Cracker people have been the subject of ridicule for centuries. Ever since these strong, independent folk made their way south into Florida both before and after the Change of Flags in 1821, they have been constantly commented upon by travelers, soldiers, and observers of all sorts. In the early nineteenth century

Cracker immigrants near Palatka c. 1880s. Photograph, Florida State Archives.

these folk were "drawn to Florida by the fertility and availability of public land, particularly in East Florida, where wild hogs and cattle were in abundance. Their livelihood consisted mainly of growing staples like corn for subsistence. Hunting and fishing supplemented their diets." But herding cattle and hogs on the open range was as important to their culture as it was to their economic survival. "Extreme mobility brought them ultimately into contact, sometimes violently, with Indians, surveyors, military officials, and even lawful purchasers of lands they squatted on. Florida's 'plain folk,' like their kinsmen in other Southern states, shared a strong adherence to popular democracy, a hatred of Indians, and a strong sense of racial superiority over blacks, whom they believed fit only for slavery. Their strong sense of individualism and resolve came from living on the isolated frontier. They usually acted on their own authority, often showing little respect for governmental or judicial authority."[1]

But if this crude image identifies many Florida Crackers, this rural civilization sometimes bred a straightforward, unobtrusive persona that can be counted among the best of American traits. In words that lend large meaning to Florida's rural folk, W. J. Cash has written in his classic commentary of the South and its people, "All the way down the line, there was a softening and gentling of the heritage of the backwoods. In every degree the masses took on under their slouch, a sort of unkept politeness an ease of port, which rendered them definitely superior, in respect of manner, to their peers in the rest of the country."[2] And still, the pervasive effects of Florida's frontier, as depicted by such writers as Marjorie Kinnan Rawlings, Marjorie Stoneman Douglas, and Patrick Smith, lingered long into the twentieth century and continued to shape the lives of Florida's Crackers.

No serious work on Florida's "Plain Folk" can address the subject of crackers without addressing the images of these folk as they were depicted by contemporaries. Not all, but most of these images were negative. And that speaks to the value of this work, for Mr. Ste.Claire not only addresses this ridicule, but also reminds us that their statements say as much about the speakers as they do about their subjects. Ste.Claire deserves much credit for taking on such a controversial subject. The term "Cracker" is so volatile these days. Many native Floridians are justifiably sensitive and angry about their past being either forgotten or disparaged. Many, particularly the older folks who remember when "cracker" was synonymous with "white trash,"are naturally suspicious of attempts by natives or newcomers to define, explain, or characterize their history or their culture. The term "Cracker" is so laden with negative images that to even use the term is to court angry stares. Some blacks equate the term with white racism. Some native Southerners resent the way the term has been used to disparage them.

The obvious pitfalls, risks, but also great value of Ste.Claire's work, reminds me of a brief encounter I had with a gentleman in north Florida after one of my Cracker programs. I could tell he had many of these same concerns and was none too happy with me for using some of the negative observations Ste.Claire also uses in this volume. His concern was that these negative images only reinforced the stereotypical, incorrect, and jaundiced view of native Floridians held by many of the newcomers in the audience. After explaining to him what I felt was the importance of exploring our history—both its negative and positive traits, warts and all—I felt as though I had won him over. His note to me several days later suggested that after some reflection I had gotten through. In a letter which I still treasure, he stated that he "would not touch the word 'Cracker' with a ten-foot pole," but added that he "admire[d my] coming to grips with it."

In such a climate discussing such a thing as the "Cracker Culture in Florida History" is not easy. It involves some risk. (Witness the recent controversy over the naming of schools, parks etc.) But that is in part why this work will be both valuable and meaningful for large numbers of people who live in Florida today.

Even among historians, especially those eager to write about oppressed ethnic groups, the Scotch-Irish antecedents of many of the Crackers have been marginalized, but mainly disparaged, as unworthy of serious attention. Witness the hail of criticism which met Grady McWhiney's seminal *Cracker Culture: Celtic Ways in the Old South* (Tuscaloosa, 1988), the first scholarly attempt to study Crackers since Frank L. Owsley's path-breaking *Plain Folk of the Old South* (Baton Rouge, 1949). One reviewer of McWhiney's work even implied that Crackers have no culture worthy of study. Other similar nonsense greeted this excellent, readable, and imaginative study.

And yet today, in some circles, "Cracker" is chic. Everybody wants to be one. Even Governor Lawton Chiles, no doubt proud of his cracker roots, is eager to employ simple, direct cracker vernacular to disarm his sophisticated opponents. The man who seems to have appropriated the mantle "He-Coon" from Panhandle Congressman Bob Sikes, revels in phrases like, "That dog won't hunt," and "I never roll up my britches until I get to the creek"—and of course the unforgettable—"The He-Coon walks just before the light of day." These "Crackerisms" conjure up rich images of rural Florida. They also speak to the understated wisdom of many of Florida's early settlers. If these phrases and sayings give us pause to reflect on contemporary problems that face our state, they also speak volumes to the many challenges, complexities, and uncertainties that continue to perplex the human condition.

If writing about Crackers in a thoughtful, meaningful way has its risks and pitfalls, it also has its rewards. We should all be glad that Dana Ste.Claire took on the task. In doing so he may have unconsciously followed the admonitions of my grandfather: "Don't worry about the mule going blind, son, just load the wagon."

NOTES

1. James M. Denham, *A Rogue's Paradise: Crime and Punishment in Antebellum Florida*, 1821-1861 (Tuscaloosa, 1997), p. 10.

2. W. J. Cash, *The Mind of the South* (New York, 1941), p.p. 72-73.

3. Journal of Southern History 55 (August 1989), p. 490.

Dr. James M. Denham is a Professor of History at Florida Southern College and is the state's foremost scholar in the areas of Cracker history and culture. He has authored numerous publications on the Antebellum South and 19th century and 20th century life in Florida, including his most recent book, "A Rogue's Paradise: Crime and Punishment in Antebellum Florida, 1821 - 1861" (Tuscaloosa: University of Alabama Press, 1997).

Foreword

by Rick Tonyan

Cattle drives. Range wars. Gunfights in trail towns. Rustlers and assorted other outlaws.

All of the above has become the subject for at least hundreds, probably thousands, of historians and mythologizers of the American West.

But none of the above exclusively belongs to the Western chroniclers.

Every subject that ever has come up in Western history or fiction also confronts myself and a handful of writers who deal with Florida's frontier. Now, with this book, Dana Ste.Claire joins our all-too-small group.

Florida's past contains all the action, drama and color of the West that has been recorded by everyone from Ned Buntline to J. Frank Dobie. It's just that few people ever have heard about it.

Maybe Florida's history should be called the Lost Frontier.

Once, I conducted an experiment to see exactly how badly lost Florida's frontier past has become. I was speaking to a civic group in Crescent City, a small town about 80 miles south of Jacksonville. During my talk, I asked for a show of hands on how many there had heard about the Gunfight at the OK Corral in Tombstone, Arizona, about 1,300 miles away from the meeting site. Virtually everybody knew at least something about that shootout, in which Wyatt Earp, his two brothers and Doc Holiday gunned down several members of the Clanton and McLaury families.

Then I asked how many at the meeting had heard about the Gunfight at McGrady's Grove on January 29, 1869. That shootout climaxed a feud between two families, the Braddocks and the Turners, over grazing rights. Three Braddock brothers squared off against three Turner brothers in the grove. After 90 seconds of gunplay, one Braddock and two Turners were killed and the other three participants were wounded.

Crescent City is within two miles of the site of McGrady's Grove. But only one man at the meeting had heard of the gunfight. And he was an in-law of the Braddocks.

If I had been speaking to a civic group in Tombstone, I'm positive more people than in-laws of the Clantons, McLaurys, Earps and Holiday would have heard about the OK Corral affair.

To add to the irony, McGrady's Grove actually was the more dramatic gunfight. If nothing else, at least all accounts agree that all the Turners and Braddocks were armed and shooting. At least one, possibly two, of the Clanton-McLaury faction were unarmed when the Earps and Holiday started firing.

The McGrady's grove gunfight was anything but an isolated incident. Guns, knives and nooses settled disputes in early Florida at least as often as lawyers and judges.

Florida's frontier was much like the West's. It just started here sooner — with the Spanish settlements in the 1500s — and lasted longer — until the closing of the open range in 1949. Out West, the Spanish began raising cattle about 100 years later and most range land closed a good 50 years earlier.

Anything that Western history or fiction had to offer could be found in Florida. Want stories about tough cow towns? Look into the annuals of Arcadia in Southwest Florida. During the 1890s, Arcadia averaged 50 gun or fist fights per day. That action was all part of a thirty year war between cattlemen and rustlers along the ironically named Peace River.

Then there was the Jackson County War from 1869-1871 in North Florida. That one saw about 150 men, women and children gunned down in fights and ambushes.

About the only thing the West had over Florida was the length of its cattle drives. For example, the Chisholm Trail from Texas to Kansas stretched about a thousand miles. Most Florida drives were no longer than 150 miles.

But neither cattle nor men on the Chisholm Trail ever were threatened by alligators.

Another bit of frontier trivia: What was the longest, bloodiest and costliest Indian War ever fought by U.S. troops?

It wasn't any of the several campaigns against Apaches or Sioux or any of the other Western tribes that have been immortalized in books and films. It was the Second Seminole War of 1835 to 1842. Seven years that cost the United States $20 million and the lives of 1,500 soldiers. Nobody knows how many civilians or Seminoles were killed.

At least most people know something about the Second Seminole War. Ask folks, even those living in the state, about Florida history. Most will reply with something about the Seminoles fighting to stay on their land and about Juan Ponce de Leon discovering Florida while looking for the Fountain of Youth.

And, that's about all anybody knows until the real estate boom of the 1920s and the modern era of development.

Those who want to fill in the gaps in their knowledge of Florida history will get a lot of help from Ste.Claire's history of Crackers.

A great deal of Florida's unheralded history is the story of the pioneering Crackers. From the late 1700s until the early 1900s, they were about the only Caucasian inhabitants in the interior of the state. They were often poor, sometimes lawless, but almost always courageous.

Crackers herded the cattle, farmed the land, cut the timber, fished the waters, and distilled the turpentine. They opened the way for industries long years before Northerners saw profit potential in the state.

Much of the blood spilled in the state came from Crackers. They fought Seminoles, Yankees and each other to establish themselves on the frontier. Crackers survived despite tropical disease, hurricanes, rattlers, cottonmouths, gators, panthers and a variety of other hazards that Nature threw in their way.

But, for the most part, Crackers have been treated as unwanted branches on Florida's family tree. The powers-that-be in the state, whether Spanish, British or American, either ignored them or referred to them in derogatory terms. Even today, in some parts of the state, "Cracker" is synonymous with "poor white trash."

Ste.Claire is one of the few in the state who has given this often maligned group their just dues. Crackers aren't only a part of Florida history. To a great extent, they *are* Florida history.

Rick Tonyan, a free-lance writer, lives in DeLeon Springs, Florida. He is the author of a variety of newspaper and magazine articles on the state's history. He also wrote "Guns of the Palmetto Plains" (Pineapple Press, 1994), a historical novel about Florida cattlemen during the War Between the States. It has been described as a "Cracker Western."

Rick Tonyan on his horse Rowdy.

Introduction

"I am content to define history as the past events of which we have knowledge and refrain from worrying about those of which we have none - until, that is, some archaeologist digs them up."

— BARBARA W. TUCHMAN, AMERICAN HISTORIAN (1912 - 1989)

I was once told, in a matter-of-fact, you-really-ought-to-know-this-sort-of-thing way, that I was a Florida Cracker - by right, I suppose - because I was a born and bred Florida native, raised in what was then the sleepy horsetown of Ocala. Now, while I didn't object to the label - and I never have - I felt the whole thing begged for some greater berth, so I offered up this footnote:

Being born in Florida doesn't necessarily make you a Florida Cracker. Indigenousness is not a prerequisite. I know plenty of native Floridians who don't know the first thing about being a Cracker and, conversely, some of the purist Florida Crackerfolk I've known in my lifetime were reared in the New York countryside.

I think I even added some of John Keasler's "a Cracker is inclined to gamble, and knows when it's going to rain" folk adage, at which point the matter became more confusing to the person I was trying to enlighten. Pressed to explain just what makes a Cracker a Cracker, I spouted a long list of Cracker traits, describing carefully what I thought were common threads binding all Crackerfolk. Finally, out of frustration with my inability to put together a clear definition of what a Cracker was, I uttered the word *culture*, a fall back to my anthropology training, I suppose, but a thought which made all the sense in the world at the time, and continues to.

I was not the first to entertain such a notion, that Cracker describes a real culture, not a social or economic condition, or a caricatured lifestyle. Frank L. Owsley, in his pioneering *Plain Folk of the Old South* (1949), outlines the cultural distinctiveness of Southerners, and Grady McWhiney in *Cracker Culture* (1988) fine-tunes Owsley's view as it relates to the Celtic ethnicity widely represented in early settlers of the South. In Florida, two notable works opened the door for scholars to study the Cracker peoples as a genuine cultural group. James M. Denham's *Florida Historical Quarterly* piece, "The Florida Cracker Before the Civil War as Seen through Traveler's Accounts" (1994), was the first work to present the Florida Cracker in a serious light by examining, among other things, the cultural traits of antebellum period white settlers. James Denham will tell you that he had a difficult time convincing fellow historians of the validity of such a study, and it was only after a letter of endorsement from Grady McWhiney that critics understood its landmark importance. And his determined effort paid off - numerous subsequent books on various aspects of Florida history cite his work, including Michael Gannon's *The New History of Florida* (Gainesville, 1996) which includes an entry on the Cracker culture written by Daniel Schafer, and Canter Brown's *Ossim Bingley Hart: Florida's Loyalist Reconstruction Governor* (Baton Rouge, 1997). Of great merit, too, is Bucuvalas, Bulger, and Kennedy's profile of Cracker life in southern Florida (*South Florida Folklife*, Jackson, 1994) which is, to my knowledge, the first ethnographic treatment of a regional population of Crackers anywhere.

The Cracker Culture in Florida History builds on these two later works - James Denham's introduction of the Florida Cracker as a worthy scholarly subject, and Bucuvalas, Bulger, and Kennedy's cultural study of South Florida Crackers. Here, an attempt is made to expand Denham's definition and the South Florida model in a broader light, through a general cultural study of Florida Cracker peoples, a sweeping ethnography of sorts. It is a perusal through the culture, offering a sampling of what makes a Cracker a Cracker, and what makes the culture a viable one. At another level, it is a call to finally lay to rest the ignorant hayseed image that Crackers have been saddled with so unjustly. Somewhere along the way, the lowly Cracker was cast out on the historical fringe by gentry scholars, and since has been treated as the red-headed step-child of Florida history. Perhaps it is time we reeled him back in, gave him a long overdue pat on the head, and began to look at the important contributions he has made to the cultural and historical development of the state.

A late 19th century image of a Southern immigrant. From Harper's New Monthly Magazine, *September 1879.*

may very well have known the ideal Cracker. His name was Herbert Kinsey, and if anyone ever embodied the spirit of Crackerness, it was this Florida backwoodsman. Herbert - somewhere in his early fifties in the late 1960s, but weathered well beyond his years - lived just east of a little nook of a town called Scrambletown in the Ocala National Forest. The town got its colorful name from its moonshining days when still operators "scrambled" from the revenuers making unannounced visits. Today, Scrambletown is a serene forest village, with seldom a social blemish.

Cracker houses like this one can be found throughout the Ocala National Forest. Photograph, Florida State Archives.

You could get to Herbert's place from the main road, but most who needed to get there from the north forest used an old Civil War period road which came in through the woods over Eaton Creek. The dirt road opened into an eerie stand of dead longleaf pines which wrapped around and hovered over Herbert's house. No one could explain why the trees had died, but it was rumored that the Kinsey place was homesteaded on sacred Indian grounds.

The house that Herbert and his wife lived in was a hand-fashioned log and frame cabin with an aging metal roof. Herbert built it himself, and modified it many times afterward. Inside, everything smelled of smoke from a hearth fire that seemed to never go out, and antlers and leather tack hung everywhere on crude hand-hewn poles and beams, each with hardened drips and pools of pine sap. Rain-catching gray graniteware pots were stepped around like furniture. Occasionally, the pots were emptied out through a front door which stayed open most of the time, and then carefully put back in their exact same places. I suppose this strategy was easier than climbing up on a flimsy roof and patching unpatchable tin.

A rusty pitcher-pump spilled water onto a front porch table basin and the bathroom was an unsteady, swing-door, one-seater outhouse which I was afraid to use. And that was it for amenities, unless you counted the fast-tacked clapboard smokehouse in the back and the two overly repaired rocking chairs on the front porch, both with ancient and worn green cushions.

Mrs. Kinsey - I never called her by her first name - cooked on an old cast-iron wood-burning stove, and I remember eating things like swamp cabbage and potatoes, and grits and very dry cornbread for lunch and dinner. I once watched her clean an Eaton Creek cooter like she was snapping a bowl of peas, hardly glancing at the poor creature while she talked to me from her rocker. I ate that several times with the Kinseys, along with frog legs, gar fish, wild rabbit and gopher tortoise - and sometimes deer that they collected from the local highways when word came fast from the local Count's Store about a fresh roadkill. This all seemed natural to everyone, especially to those who could keep themselves alive for a month or so on the meat from a single deer.

Herbert made a little money doing mostly odd jobs throughout most of the year. Among other things, he picked deer tongue from the forest and sold overstuffed croaker sacks full of it for a few dollars, back when the plant was used as a tobacco additive. I don't recall ever seeing the buyer, but people talked about him as if he was there with money every day. Every once in a while Herbert would barter vegetables from his truck garden, though most of these were grown for home

Scrambletown's own Herbert Kinsey in his trademark Willys jeep on the grounds of the Youth Conservation Camp. Photograph taken in the summer of 1967 by the late Denver Ste.Claire, Sr.

consumption. And although I heard once that he worked a still, I never saw a trace of it.

Around all of this and during the summers of the 1960s, Herbert worked as a superintendent for my father Denver Ste.Claire, who was director of the nearby Youth Conservation Camp. When they crossed paths, and they often did, the two would sometimes talk for hours about life and living, environmental preservation, garbage routes, fishing, an unrepairable Lake Eaton fishing dock, and food, among many other things. I remember at every meeting, my father would always ask Herbert if everything was o.k., and if he needed anything, and Herbert would say, with a nearly-toothless smile, that things were "just fine, just dandy, Mr. Ste.Claire." He was poor, but very proud. My father trusted and respected Herbert, as did everyone, and it was for this reason that I was frequently placed in his care for the day, riding around with him in the Army-surplus jeep the Camp provided him for the summer. Herbert taught me how to drive in that old Willys.

While it was a lot for a youngster to take in, Herbert taught me a great deal about life. With his usually evenly-presented, but sometimes animated stories, from a face that had the look and color of worn leather, he helped shape the outlook and philosophy of a youngster who only thought he was tagging along in life. Along the way, I was able to sample the Cracker way firsthand and the experience became deeply imprinted. I realized this years later when I found myself quickly defending the Cracker when the word was used as a slur for poor white trash or for Southern bigots, or when I would catch myself espousing some clarification on how lake crawdaddies and cooter were eaten, or how swamp cabbage was taken and prepared.

It might be said that I carry some Cracker heritage in that I have been captured by the spirit of Crackers many times in my life, including those who lived around Scrambletown in the 1960s and early 1970s, and those who are acquaintances today. But I am not, by right or proxy, a Cracker, although I would be proud to say I was one, if I was. In my mind, to be Cracker, you must be a part of the culture, you must live the Cracker life. Only a real Cracker fully understands this.

Sadly, the once-widespread Cracker culture seems to be dissipating. Like the worn Cracker houses that once speckled the Florida landscape, the purist form of the Cracker culture is coming apart in bits and pieces, lost in a fast-paced society that has finally stuck its arm into the remote backwoods of the state. One goal of this work is to record at least some of this rapidly disappearing Cracker heritage, and the lengthy history of it. At times, it is written with an anthropological slant, but this is only a reflection of how I was taught to observe and record human behavior.

Today, the Cracker culture is interpreted liberally. It has become a convenient catch-all for many things that really have little or nothing to do with the culture proper, like a rodeo, a corn-eating contest, or a literary reading - or even a fair exhibit that displays fancy parlor stoves, expensive farm equipment, and other "pioneer" antiques, things Crackers rarely used back then, simply because they could hardly afford to. But some would say that this is the "new" Cracker culture; others see it as an unfortunate by-product of assimilation.

A second goal of this work is to present a sampling of the real Cracker culture, from the foods Crackers ate to the houses they built, so that the reader can garner thoughts on what makes a Cracker a Cracker. The profile of the Cracker culture presented in this book is a patchwork of many things: oral histories and opinions from the mouths of Crackers themselves - present and past - accounts, some obscure, from observers of the early culture, perspectives from contemporary writers on the subject, and bits and pieces of pertinent literary excerpts, all arranged and stitched together in a tidy, but not too busy, quasi-anthropological pattern. The object here is to touch on everything Cracker, but not to belabor any single point (for those who seek more information about a particular Cracker topic, a select reading list follows each chapter). But surely there are many things relative to the culture which I have missed and for this, I beg the pardon of Crackers everywhere.

Cracker women were responsible for a great deal of work on the homestead, including tending livestock, gardening, performing household chores, and raising children. From Harper's New Monthly Magazine, *1881.*

What's a Cracker?

"There is no easy definition for a Florida Cracker. The literal-minded say he is simply a Florida-born native. This has nothing whatsoever to do with it. A man can be a Yankee and a Cracker in the same lifetime, although it is true only a limited number of men are equipped to do this. Most of these, however, end up as Crackers. The rest wonder all their lives what is wrong... The term is not easy to define. You are or you aren't. A Cracker is inclined to gamble, and knows when it's going to rain."

—JOHN KEASLER, *SURROUNDED ON THREE SIDES*.

As ageless as the Cracker culture is the mystery of who these hardy settlers were and how they became known as Crackers. Remarkably, more is known about the lifestyles of Crackers through two centuries than the historical development of the word *cracker,* a term that seems so befitting for the backwoods-savvy culture it describes, yet one which continues to baffle people everywhere, even Florida Crackers.

That Florida-born natives, mostly rural folks, have come to be known as Crackers in recent years has little to do with the word's meaning, in that migrating Northerners and out-of-staters comprised some of the earliest and hardiest Cracker stock in the state.

Today, scores of journalists and historians continue to struggle with the meaning of *cracker*, while others seem to subscribe to generalized definitions of the word. Occasionally, a determined journalist will tackle the problem, like newspaper writer Robert Hunter. In a column entitled, "'Cracker research leaves few sure answers," Hunter explores the meaning of the term but, in doing so, also exposes the confusion surrounding it: "Nowhere did I discover expert witness discussion of what I was looking for - how come our English word "cracker" was applied to these particular people who so commonly are described by us as "Cracker."[1]

A reader later tries to assist Hunter: "The definition of Florida Cracker that I heard when I went to DeLand in 1932, not long after Hunter arrived in Daytona

Beach (in 1925), was that the term referred to "corn cracker" of whom there were many operating in the Florida backwoods, especially in Volusia County. 'Corn crackers' were moonshiners who used cracked corn mash, which after fermentation, they distilled into 'white lightning' which freely flowed at election campaign rallies of that time."[2]

The reader's interpretation of the word *cracker* illustrates some of the well-entrenched folklore that surrounds it, and provides one of several enduring, and colorful, theories on the origin of the word, all of which come with various doses of historical validity. Southern folk etymology traces the term to two popular explanations of the word: that *cracker* was derived from the sound of a cracking whip, or that it alludes to the cracking of dry corn by poor southerners who relied on ground corn as a chief dietary staple. But, there are literally dozens of theories on how the word came to be. Some of these have become finely woven into the popular folk fabric of Florida, while others are more exotic. Here are some of the more conventional:

Whip Crackers - Florida Crackers nowadays spend a great deal of time trying to persuade themselves and others that the term *cracker* originated from the sound of whips cracking over cattle or teams of oxen or mules, believing that all of their antecedents were drovers. This is by far the most popular

"A Florida Cracker in Excitement." Pencil sketch by Henry J. Morton, 1867. From St. Augustine, 1867: Drawings by Henry J. Morton, *edited and annotated by Thomas Graham. Published by The St. Augustine Historical Society, 1996.*

theory for the origin of *cracker*, and surely the most embellished. Contemporary Cracker cowmen will tell you the same, that the word alludes to the gunshot popping of whips which accompanied cattle drives, made by cowhunters skilled at cracking rawhide whips. To some, and to an end less glamorous, the whips were those of poor migrants from Alabama, Georgia and Carolina who drove their livestock down the country roads of Florida in the 19th century. John Lambert's *Travels Through Lower Canada, and the United States of North America*, published in 1810, is the earliest known reference to the term *cracker* as originating from the sound of a popping whip: "The wagoners are familiarly

An early Cracker cowhunter whip on a cabbage palm. Photograph by Roger Simms, 1997.

called *crackers*, from the smacking of their whip, I suppose." Later, an entry in the Boston Beacon of June 11, 1887 notes the same: "The word *Cracker*... is supposed to have been suggested by their cracking whips over oxen or mules in taking their cotton to the market."

Carl Allen in his *Root Hog or Die Poor* offers a variation of the whip cracker theory: "The word 'cracker' applied to the Florida-born people comes from the rawhide whip, or drag, as the ol' cowhunters called them. Apparently when this part of the country began to finally get settled and Mr. Plant and Mr. Flagler had pushed their railroads into this land of palmetto and flat land, the young cow hunters would drive their scrub cows up close to the train and the people who were coming down here to buy land would say, 'See the young men cracking their whips.' Now on the end of the whips was a small strip of buckskin called a 'cracker,' so they begin to say that there were some more of those Florida crackers; thus came the words 'Florida cracker.'"[3]

Cowhunter historian Joyce Peters offers an interesting insight on the luxury of owning whips, and why they should have nothing to do with the naming of Crackers: "These poor people (Crackers) had no leather for shoes, much less cow whips which promoters are using to explain the term 'cracker.'

Corncrackers - The theory relating to corncracking is popular among many rural Floridians, especially those near the Georgia border. It holds that the word originated from the cracking of dry corn by backwoods people who were too poor to buy finer grains. The nickname Georgia Cracker is believed to have evolved from the term corncracker, one who cracks or pulverizes corn to make grits or cornmeal, and it is in this sense that the "Cracker State" motto has been used to describe Georgia since post-Civil War times. Folk etymologist Stuart Flexner elaborates: "Such corn cracking was a common chore in all the colonies (and) corn remained a basic cereal in the South long after the North had

> *"Well, people didn't know what cracker meant and they thought it was just a slang word, you know, for a person. But it was named after the whip, I think, the crackin' whip, as the cowhunters come in. There wasn't cowboys in those days, there was cowhunters, and they used those whips and we'd say, "Yep, here comes the Crackers." That's where the word comes from. I'm always a callin' myself a Cracker."*
>
> — JESSE OTIS BEALL, DEBARY,
> FLORIDA CRACKER, 1997.

turned to other grains - that's why cracker had come to mean a southern backwoods-man by 1836, and a poor white from Georgia or Florida by 1891."[4] Emily P. Burke in her *Reminiscences of Georgia* (1850) could very well have started all of this when she wrote that some Georgians were called Crackers "from the circumstance that they formerly pounded all their corn, which is their principal article of diet."

Biscuit Crackers - There is some truth to the notion that the term *cracker* may have been derived, at least in some areas of the South, from the baked and edible variety of cracker. Cracker western author Rick Tonyan notes that, following the Civil War, carpetbaggers witnessed many Southern white settlers too poor to eat anything but hardtack, and because of this, called the migrants

Late 19th century cracker tin. It is not very likely that soda wafers had anything to do with the naming of Crackers. Photograph by Roger Simms, 1997.

Crackers. Cowhunter historian Joyce Peters offers a convincing explanation of this: "The crackers had a difficult time getting cheap food. At the mills throughout the south, the first ground corn was the cheapest, because it had only one process. The meal could be made at home, also, with the oldest method on earth: stone ground. However they could come by this meal, it would be mixed with whatever they had ... water, lard, etc. It could be baked outdoors on a rock by a fire. The baked product was referred to as a cracker. They took this in their travels because it was easily kept in a sack and it was edible as is or boiled in a stew. When the wealthy saw these people camped (it was assumed that) this was a staple of their existence." [5] Allen Morris' *Florida Place Names* notes that the Cracker Swamp in Duval County was named so for an unusual cache of goods it once held. After the Battle of Olustee on February 20, 1864, Confederate soldiers found an abandoned Union railway boxcar near Baldwin filled with some 400 boxes of hard biscuits or crackers. From that day on, the branch of McGirts Creek over which the railroad crossed has been known as Cracker Swamp.[6]

Crackerbox Houses - This theory is heard every now and then. It holds that crackers got their name from the simple crackerbox-shaped cabins in which they lived.

"A Florida Log Cabin." Drawing from original 19th century photograph by Earnest A. Meyer. From Pen Drawings of St. Augustine and Other Views of Florida *by E. A. Meyer, 1940. From the collection of The St. Augustine Historical Society.*

Quaker - In his 1877 description of Florida Crackers, Samuel Fairbanks suggests the term may have been derived from the Spanish word *cuáquero*, meaning a Quaker, making reference to a colony of Quakers which earlier settled in Florida.[7] Noted folklorist Stetson Kennedy offers the same explanation: "These (early 19th century) 'bad characters' were the forerunners of American civilization, and it was they who acquired the name 'cracker' which even then was applied to the poor white folk of Florida, Georgia, and Alabama. Probably the true story about how the crackers got their name is that when their 'bad character' forebears first began to filter into Florida they were quite naturally called cuácaros (Quakers) by the Spaniards, and it was a simple matter, phonetically, for the Anglo-Saxons to conclude that they were being called 'crackers.'"[8]

The American lexicon has been all over the field in trying to define the word *cracker*. Robert Hendrickson's *Whistlin' Dixie: A Dictionary of Southern*

Expressions notes that the word is synonymous with a poor white person so called from their use of cracked corn.[9] To this, the *Dictionary of Epithets and Terms of Address* adds that the word in the United States is used to describe a southern rustic as well as a poor white person.[10] *Webster's New World Dictionary of American English* agrees, but adds that it is a contemptuous term for both. It gets worse. Hugh Rawson's *Wicked Words* describes a

"A 'Terminus' Rough." From The Great South *by Edward King, 1875, p. 206.*

cracker as a low-down Southern white,[11] and the *Random House Historical Dictionary of American Slang* appends this with ignorant, brutal, loutish and bigoted.[12]

Snodgrass, in her *Illustrated Dictionary of Little-Known Words from Literary Classics*, piles on the pejorative: "cracker is a derogatory term for an ignorant or illiterate southern white bigot, especially a smart-mouthed, boastful, or swaggering rural racist who often exacerbates local disharmony or brutalizes, menaces, or takes advantage of nonwhite neighbors."[13] All this for the lowly Cracker.

Some anomalies persist, as well. *Grose's Classical Dictionary of the Vulgar Tongue* equates *cracker* with a person's backside[14] and Dunkling notes that *cracker* in modern British slang refers to an attractive woman.[15] As a side note, *Cracker Jack*, the snack, may have something to do with Crackers the people, but no one knows for sure. *Cracker Jack* is the brand name of a caramel-covered popcorn and peanut mixture created by a Chicago vendor named F. W. Rueckheim in the late 19th century when humorous usage of the word *cracker* was at a peak.[16]

But references to Crackers predate, by centuries in some cases, the events and social occasions which gave rise to all of these theories. Its roots are found in 16th century, if not earlier, England where the word originally meant a braggart or a fast talker. The earliest recorded use of the term as a description of a character trait appears in as 1509.[17] *Palmer's Folk Etymology* notes that the early form of *cracker* was derived from the word *crack*, or the Old English *crake*, which means to boast, a *craker* or *crakar* being a braggart or a liar.[18] The word was used in this manner by William Shakespeare in King John, c. 1595, when he wrote "What cracker is this same that deafes our eares with this abundance of superfluous breath?"

> "What is the origin of the term 'Florida Cracker?' I didn't even know the answer to that question and I am one. I am descended from tried and true Cracker stock on both sides of my family. What else could result from the union of a Jacksonville dad and a Palatka momma?"
>
> — JOHN CARTER, JOURNALIST AND FIFTH-GENERATION CRACKER FLORIDIAN. FROM HIS SUNDAY PUNCH COLUMN, *THE NEWS-JOURNAL*, AUGUST 10, 1997.

Kenneth K. Krakow explains that *cracker* is a corruption of an ancient term used in Scotland to designate a certain yeomanry class of independents who were obnoxious to the aristocracy.[19] Francis R. Goulding, in *Marooner's Island* (1869), was one of the first post-Civil War writers to suggest the Celtic origins of the word, offering that the name was an old word from earlier Scottish-Irish settlers which described a person who talked boastingly. Early on in America, the term came to represent a host of undesirable characteristics - dishonest, shiftless, and insipid, to name just a few. Whatever *cracker* may have originally implied, the term was well worn by the time cowhunters began to herd their cattle through the Florida wilds in the early 1800s.

In the mid 18th century, the term *cracker* "respecialized," and was used to characterize poor or rogue settlers of the rural south, and later, to describe a proud Florida backcountry culture. Throughout Florida's history, the meaning of the word has vacillated

> "The word cracker is burdened with several centuries' worth of bad connotations. At least when the word is applied to people instead of being served with soup."
>
> — AUTHOR RICK TONYAN IN "CRACKING UP CRACKER MYTHS," *HALIFAX MAGAZINE*, SEPTEMBER, 1997.

considerably, alternately taking on derogatory or desirable tones. Early on a racial slur for impoverished whites, *cracker* ameliorated to become a regionally affectionate term in the first part of the 20th century, and was even used to name several baseball teams in the south. Around 1914, the DeLand Crackers were among the state's earliest and best baseball teams, and the longtime nickname of a minor league team in Atlanta was the Crackers.[20] The naming of Crackertown in Levy County was a riposte to nearby Yankeetown by a proud group of west coast Crackers.[21]

But by the 1950s, the term once again became a pejorative, eroding into a racial slur for bigoted backwoods Southern whites. In many areas, the term is still generally thought of an offensive one and, in some cases, is considered a racial epithet that is a violation under the Florida Hate Crimes Act.[22] In 1991, the Highlands County School Board was embroiled in controversy over the proposed name of a new school, Cracker Trail Elementary. Many locals took offense to the name, claiming that the word *cracker* was an insult. Whites complained that it was a disparaging term for poor whites, and one black parent suggested that *cracker* was anti-black. In the end, the board decided to keep the name, pointing out that it had been derived from an important part of the community's history, the Cracker Trail, a route used by early Florida cowhunters to drive their cattle.[23]

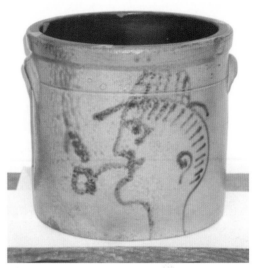

A mid-19th century two-gallon stoneware crock decorated with a caricature of a Cracker homesteader, complete with straw hat and corncob pipe. The reverse of the crock has a large C painted in the same cobalt blue slip, but it is not known if this denotes the word "Cracker." Collection of the author. Photograph by Bruce Waasdorp, Clarence, New York, 1996.

Cracker has long been a racial slur used by African Americans as a contemptuous term for the Southern white. In the early 19th century, Southern slaves and free blacks used the African word *buckras* to refer to whites, but by the mid-century *cracker* had become the preferred term.[24]

Journalist John Carter, a fifth generation Floridian of Scotch-Irish and Minorcan decent, tells of an offbeat response to one of his columns in which he proudly announced his Florida Cracker heritage. A Jewish woman, incensed at the piece, called to inform him that she had arranged a formal debate, at which time he would defend why he chose to use such an anti-Semitic remark - *cracker*

- in a newspaper story. The woman went on to insist that every Cracker despised Jewish people. All of this was news to John, but it illustrates well how convoluted the meaning of *cracker* has become.

Today, there are many Floridians who call themselves Crackers with great pride. In the 1970s, especially after the election of Georgia native Jimmy Carter

> *There are some members of the Cracker culture who remain uncomfortable with the cracker label. Florida cowhunter historian Joyce Peters, who spends a great deal of her time interpreting the Cracker lifestyle throughout the state, explains that the term, to her, has long been associated with an undesirable poor white class, something she learned painfully as a youngster. She offers this personal insight on a powerful effect of the word: "As a child playing on the banks of the St. Johns River, I was called a cracker. The woman (well-dressed and with a group of people that she was showing the river) literally spit the word at me and retreated back a few steps as if I might contaminate her. When I asked my great-grandmother, at whose house I was staying, what was a cracker, she explained to me that crackers were white people that could not help themselves. The ones she had met were from Georgia. But it would be rude also to correct someone publicly, even in order to explain. Great-granny explained the lady who used the word was not 'nice' - 'nice ladies' would not call someone that. Great-granny assured me the 'lady' did not understand that the word could hurt peoples' feelings."*

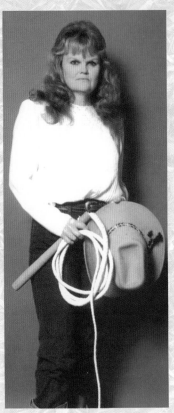

Cowhunter historian Joyce Peters.

to the presidency in 1976, many born-again Crackers emerged, proud to claim their southern heritage. Humorist Roy Blount, Jr. even titled his book about southerners in the Carter era *Crackers*.[25]

Still, there are places in the state where the word *cracker* should be used with care. Abraham Lincoln once made a statement to the effect that no matter how much you respect the common man, never call a man common to his face, and I imagine the same thing applies to Crackers in some areas. Allen Morris, writer of the longtime syndicated Florida newspaper column "Cracker Politics," suggests that it might be prudent to accompany the nickname with a smile. But while stubborn negative connotations will always be part of the cultural baggage Crackers carry with them, it is important that we begin to recognize that the term *Cracker* describes, chronologically and ethnographically, a distinct group that played an important role in the historical and cultural development of Florida and in the peopling of the lower South.

In the lengthy evolution of the word, one which spans some five centuries, timely explanations have been offered along the way for *cracker*, and many of these were convincing enough to become part of the collective American lexicon, like, for example, the adaption of the whip-cracker theory during the emergence of a cowhunter subculture in the early 1800s. Appropriately enough, University of South Florida linguistics professor Robert O'Hara refers to these convenient word associations as "horseback etymologies." Other theories never caught on. But no matter how you catalogue him or in what manner you explain him, a Cracker is a Cracker. Crackers will always be a people, a cultural group that early on provided the very foundation on which rural Florida was settled.

NOTES

1. Robert Hunter, *Daytona Beach News-Journal*, "Looking Back" column, November 3, 1996.

2. Paul E. Raymond, letter to the editor, November 26, 1996, *Daytona Beach News-Journal*.

3. Carl Allen, *Root Hog or Die Poor: Cracker Memories of Carl Allen*. Auburndale: Carl Allen's Cafe, 1996, p. 340.

4. Stuart Berg Flexner, *Listening to America: An Illustrated History of Words and Phrases from our Lively and Splendid Past*. New York: Simon and Schuster, 1982.

5. Conversation with cowhunter historian Joyce Peters, Fort Pierce, Florida, March 21, 1997.

6. Allen Morris, *Florida Place Names*. Sarasota: Pineapple Press, Inc. (1995), p. 59.

7. Samuel Fairbanks, "The Florida Cracker," *The Semi-Tropical: A Monthly Journal Devoted To Southern Agriculture, Horticulture, and To Immigration*, September 1877, p. 526.

8. Stetson Kennedy, *Palmetto Country*. Tallahassee: Florida A & M University Press, 1989, p. 59.

9. Robert Hendrickson, *Whistlin' Dixie: A Dictionary of Southern Expressions. Volume I, Dictionary of American Regional Expressions*. New York: Facts on File, 1993, p. 76.

10. Leslie Dunkling, *A Dictionary of Epithets and Terms of Address*. London: Routledge, 1990, p. 80.

11. Hugh Rawson, *Wicked Words: A Treasury of Curses, Insults, Put-Downs, and Other Formerly Unprintable Terms from Anglo-Saxon Times to the Present*. New York: Crown Publishers, Inc., 1989, p. 99.

12. Lighter, J. E., Editor, *Random House Historical Dictionary of American Slang*, Volume 1. New York: Random House, 1994, p. 503.

13. Mary Ellen Snodgrass, *An Illustrated Dictionary of Little-Known Words from Literary Classics*, Oxford: ABC-CLIO, p. 58.

14. Francis Grose, *A Classical Dictionary of the Vulgar Tongue*. New York: Dorset Press, 1992, p. 102.

15. Leslie Dunkling, *A Dictionary of Epithets and Terms of Address*. London: Routledge, 1990, p. 80.

16. Tad Tuleja, *The New York Public Library Book of Popular Americana*. New York: MacMillan, 1994, p. 82.

17. James C. Clark, "The Origin of the Florida 'Cracker.'" *Florida Magazine*, *Orlando Sentinel*, July 21, 1991.

18. Rev. A. Smythe Palmer, *Folk Etymology: A Dictionary*. New York: Greenwood Press 1969, p. 82.

19. Kenneth K. Krakow, *Georgia Place-Names*. Macon: Winship Press 1975, p. 55.

20. Jack Fortes, "Baseball was booming a century ago." *The Volusian*, September 22, 1996. Information courtesy of the West Volusia Historical Society.

21. Allen Morris, *Florida Place Names*. Sarasota: Pineapple Press, Inc. (1995), p. 59.

22. Robert Hendrickson, Whistlin' Dixie: A Dictionary of Southern Expressions. Volume I, *Dictionary of American Regional Expressions*. New York: Facts on File, 1993, p. 76.

23. James C. Clark, "The Origin of the Florida 'Cracker.'" *Florida Magazine*, *Orlando Sentinel*, July 21, 1991.

24. Charles Reagan Wilson, "Crackers" In, *Encyclopedia of Southern Culture*, Charles Reagan Wilson and William Ferris, editors. Chapel Hill: The University of North Carolina Press, 1989, p. 1132.

25. Ibid.

A 19th century caricature of a Cracker. From Harper's New Monthly Magazine.

The Cracker in Florida History

"Several idle People from Northward, some of whom are great Villains, Horse thieves ... have settled and built Huts on the Lands proposed to be ceded by the Indians to His Majesty ... You will easily distinguish, that the People I refer to are really what you and I understand by Crackers ... Persons who have no settled habitation, and live by hunting and plundering the industrious Settlers."

— LETTER FROM JAMES HABERSHAM, ACTING GOVERNOR OF GEORGIA, TO GOVERNOR JAMES WRIGHT IN LONDON, AUGUST 20, 1772.

When exactly the Cracker culture emerged in the south and diffused into Florida is difficult to say, but by the early 1700s, illegal migrants were already a problem for officials who governed La Florida, and it was probably during this period that *cracker* or a similar form of word began to be used to describe a class of people rather than a character trait. By the 1760s, *cracker* in its new form was commonly employed by the gentry class, especially those who resided in the coastal regions, as an ethnic slur for Scotch-Irish frontiersmen in the South.[1] Eighteenth century documents describe these renegade settlers as rootless, unruly, stubborn, and corrupt. To some, *cracker* and *criminal* were synonymous. During the 1760s, the term identified loosely organized gangs of horse thieves, counterfeiters, and slave-nappers - surely one of the first criminal syndicates in America. In 1767, the Rollestown settlement near present-day Palatka was described by Henry Laurens as "Mr. Rolle's crackertown," a poke at founder Denys Rolle's attempt to form his colony using English riffraff, mostly vagrants, debtors, beggars and pickpockets.[2] As author Ronald W. Haase (*Classic Cracker*, 1992) aptly puts it, "the first-generation Florida Cracker was not a pillar of society."

One of the earliest accounts of the rambunctious Crackers and their general defiance of authority is explained in a letter of June 27, 1766, from Colonial official Gavin Cochrane to the Earl of Dartmouth. In this letter, Cochrane attempts to expound the general demeanor of Crackers: "I should explain to your Lordship what is meant by Crackers; a name they have got from being great boasters; they are a lawless set of rascals on the frontiers of Virginia, Maryland, the Carolinas and Georgia, who often change their abode."[3] Apparently, the Cracker "problem" was not confined to Florida. The reference to the Cracker's habit of changing abodes alludes to their elusive manner as they were hard to find, especially when they broke the law. In 1784, the Cracker situation remained cause for concern, at least in some areas of the East, as noted by this entry in the *London Chronicle* (No. 4287): "Maryland, the back settlements of which colony had since the peace been greatly disturbed by the inroads of that hardy banditti well know by the name of Crackers."[4] The Carolina area, too, was plagued by a similar hooligan population: "I speak only of backwoodsman, not of the inhabitants in general of South Carolina ... I speak only of that *heathen race* known by the name of *Crackers*."[5]

> "(It defends against) the Insults of the Indians but also of those of a parcel of people commonly called Crackers, a set of Vagabonds often as bad or worse than the Indians themselves."
>
> — LETTER FROM MESSRS. SIMPSON AND BARNARD TO ROYAL GOVERNOR JAMES WRIGHT, DATED MARCH, 1767, EXPLAINING WHY AN INDIAN TRADING POST NEAR AUGUSTA SHOULD NOT BE ABANDONED BY THE BRITISH.

The British during their short, two-decade stay in Florida from 1763 to 1784 despised the lawless Crackers, a settler class they had not willingly invited after gaining possession of territory at the end of the Seven Years' War.[6] The Spanish evacuated the province soon after Spain ceded it to Britain, leaving Florida virtually empty. The British had ambitious plans for its East and West Florida colonies and attempted to attract settlers with offers of land grants. They were moderately successful, and people migrated into Florida. Some were loyal to the Crown and some were not. Rogue Cracker settlers began to establish themselves in the remote areas of the colonies, and here they fastly became a problem for British officials. Authorities in neighboring Georgia were worried too that these outlying

> "(They are) a special type of Anglo-American known as Crackers, or Gougers, who are nearly all one-eyed."
>
> — PRE-REVOLUTIONARY TRAVELER LOUIS LECLERC MILFORD OBSERVATION ON THE PERVASIVE RESULTS OF AN EARLY AND BARBAROUS CRACKER CODE OF JUSTICE WHICH ALLOWED FOR THE GOUGING OUT OF AN OFFENDER'S EYE. APPARENTLY, MANY 18TH CENTURY CRACKERS WERE OFFENDED BY EACH OTHER, AND JUSTICE WAS READILY SWIFT.

During the Spanish and British occupations of Florida, Cracker settlers who had little regard for the authority of the Crown were a problem for government officials. From The Great South *by Edward King, 1875.*

A Florida Cracker mounted on an ox which is pulling a covered wagon. This photograph, taken by F. A. Meyer in Moultrie, Florida in the 1880s, was later reproduced as a drawing (page 45) from the original plate by his son E. A. Meyer in his tourist folio, Supplement to Pen Drawings of St. Augustine and Other Views of Florida, *published in 1946. Meyer entitled the work, "The Lightning Express or the Team of a Florida Cracker." From the collection of the St. Augustine Historical Society.*

"Having contemplated these scenes of art and industry, my venerable host, in company with his son, conducted me to the neat habitation, which is situated in a spacious airy forest, a little distance from the river bank, commanding a comprehensive and varied prospect; an extensive reach of the river in front; on the right hand a spacious lawn or savanna; on the left the timber yard; the vast fertile low lands and forests on the river upwards; and the plantations adjoining. A cool evening arrived after a sultry day. As we approached the door, conducted by the young man, his lovely bride arrayed in native innocence and becoming modesty, with an air and smile of grace and benignity, meets and salutes us! what a Venus! What an Adonis! said I in silent transport; every action and feature seem to reveal the celestial endowments of the mind: though a native sprightness and sensibility appear, yet virtue and discretion direct and rule. The dress of this beauteous sylvan queen was plain but clean, neat and elegant, all of cotton, and of her own spinning and weaving."

— Quaker naturalist William Bartram overcome by Cracker deities near Savannah, April of 1776, in his *Travels Through North & South Carolina, Georgia, East & West Florida.*

areas would be occupied by frontiersmen who had no allegiance to the Crown and who would eventually cause them great trouble. This concern is illustrated by a letter of 1771 from Governor Wright who advised against granting land to settlers of the "Back Parts of the Province of Georgia," because he feared the backwoods would become a "Kind of Asylum for Offenders who will fly from justice ... And that in Process of time (and Perhaps no great Distance) they will become formidable Enough, to Oppose His Majesty's Authority ... And throw everything into Confusion."[7]

> *"Such measures may perhaps seem unnecessary to those who have never had to deal with the character of the majority of adjacent Americans, especially those who dwell in the interior of the southern states and who are called Crackers, a species of white renegade."*
>
> — MANUEL DE ZESPEDES, SPANISH GOVERNOR OF EAST FLORIDA, IN A LETTER OF JUNE 20, 1790.

Lands ceded by the Indians and British campaigns brought a steady flow of settlers to the lower South in the late 18th century, many of whom homesteaded without proper authority. Delma Presley has identified several points of infusion as well as routes of migration by settlers into and through Georgia, and it can be assumed that these same routes carried Crackers farther south into Florida in the late 1700s: "The dominant current was the Scotch-Irish of

E.A Meyer   **The Lightning Express, or the Team of a Florida Cracker**   Photo 1875

45

Northern Ireland who entered Georgia from North and South Carolina, for the most part; they were a part of a larger tide of immigration which swept southward from Pennsylvania, Maryland, and Virginia, and merged with others who had landed at ports on the coasts of North and South Carolina, particularly at Charlestown harbor. The new population also included English, Welsh, French, and German settlers."[8] It is clear that during this period there was a substantial "increase by the accession of the Crackers from the Provinces," as British Justice Anthony Stokes describes it in a letter of 1783. Stokes also notes that the Crackers conducted themselves like the "Tartars of Asia" in overtaking the planters along the coasts.

> *"(The Crackers) came into Florida from the far ends of Georgia and the Carolina during the Revolutionary War ... planted but little corn and made up the deficiency with whortle berries, blackberries and starvation."*
>
> — GEORGE C. CLARK,
> EARLY 1800s FLORIDA TRAVELER.

More is known about the Crackers during the subsequent Second Spanish period (1784 - 1821) as greater numbers of the vagabond settlers came into contact with Spanish residents. This diffusion of Crackers is explained well by historian James A. Lewis: "In the eighteenth century, the Anglo-American population constantly pushed the (Spanish) border ever further south and west. In many ways, Spanish residents along this border had more contact with English-speaking frontiersmen than did the inhabitants of older English settlements along the eastern seaboard. It is not surprising, hence, that Spanish officials wrote about crackers. These officials had to deal with the aggressive behavior of their neighbors."[9]

By the mid 1700s, a class of rogue white settlers in the South was referred to as Crackers. From The Great South *by Edward King, 1875.*

46

During the Second Spanish period, Manuel de Zespedes, an experienced Spanish officer who served as governor of East Florida from 1784 to 1790, offered a plan to control the nomadic and anarchical backwoodsmen during a turbulent period for his Spanish colony. His lengthy report of June 20, 1790 is one of the earliest, if not the first Spanish document to officially employ the word *cracker*. Zespedes, frustrated with the reckless lifestyle of mavericks in his territory, wrote, "These crackers are nomadic like Arabs and are distinguished from savages only in their color, language and superiority of their depraved cunning and untrustworthiness."

The retiring governor's sweeping critique of Crackers was somewhat well-intentioned, though, as his objective was to help Spanish officials understand the anarchical settlers better so that they could bend them to the crown's interest. Zespedes' mission is interpreted in a letter of introduction from Cuban governor Luis de las Casas written August 14, 1790: "His purpose is to demonstrate the need to complete settling the St. Marys River, a site that Zespedes considers vital for the preservation of that province (East Florida). Populating the area will impede the influx of rootless people called Crackers, whose immigration will surely occur if the area is abandoned. Their presence will cause further embarrassments."[10]

> *"(They are) vagabonds coming to Florida at the middle of the 1700s ... An improvident and lawless set of paupers from the frontiers of Virginia, Maryland, the Carolinas, and Georgia, often as bad or worse than the Indians. Generally gaunt, pale and leather skinned, they appeared to know neither necessity nor desire, but only silent, joyless, painless existence, which is perfect in its way as a tree or stone. Their improvidence, however, was cheered frequently by drunkenness and fornication; the perpetual presence of their destitution was alleviated by an absence of moral standards; and inasmuch as no form of law coerced Crackers, any divergence of opinion could be terminated, quickly and healthfully, with the fist."*
>
> — BRANCH CABELL AUTHORED THIS UNFLATTERING ACCOUNT OF FLORIDA CRACKERS IN THE EARLY 1800S FROM JAMES DENHAM'S "THE FLORIDA CRACKER BEFORE THE CIVIL WAR AS SEEN THROUGH TRAVELERS' ACCOUNTS," 1994.

Writing from St. Augustine, Zespedes provided remarkable detail in his report, offering a rare profile of the Cracker living in Florida during the late 18th century:

"As skilled as the Indians in hunting, willing to dare immense rivers with fragile rafts or to track man and animal through the densest forests, these (Crackers) erect Indian-style huts in the first unpopulated space fit to grow corn that they stumble upon in order to give shelter to their wives and children. Once done, they move again, always keeping themselves beyond the reach of all civilized law. In the land vacated by these crackers, other less antisocial groups take their place. But like their predecessors, these individuals are also enemies of all civil control and generally lack the rudiments of any religious morality whatsoever. This second class of crackers likewise tends to abandon their homes upon the approach of a third type of settler. Although this third wave deigns to ask and receive legal title to the land, even they give obedience to their mother republic only when they feel like it.

The desire of the first three classes of *crackers* to escape all legal authority is so strong that they prefer to live in Indian or better still, Spanish territory rather than live under the gentle yoke of civilized society - all this at the price of exposing themselves to the unspeakable horrors of war with the savages, of seeing their crops frequently destroyed, their homes burnt, and their families slain in the most excruciatingly cruel fashion." [11]

Crackers continued to arrived on the Florida frontier during the late Spanish period as their incursion into the Spanish territory was encouraged by the United States, just as England had done before. This widescale seizure of Spanish lands by foreign groups was a concern of many Spanish authorities, including Zespedes: "These states are motivated by the desire to expand their frontiers and ultimately to gain control over the vacant and foreign land that the *crackers* continue to usurp. There can be no doubt, consequently, that Georgia fomented and aided, at first secretly and them later openly, the invasion that

> *"Dirty, ragged and dusty, seated upon long-tailed and short-eared horses, with the deadly rifle resting in front, and a short jacket, long beard and hair and a broad brim hat"*
>
> — JOHN T. SPRAGUE, A SECOND SEMINOLE WAR SOLDIER DESCRIBES AN ENCOUNTER WITH A FLORIDA CRACKER, LATE 1830S.

> *"(Crackers are) pine-landers ... the most degraded race of human beings claiming an Anglo-Saxon origin that can be found on the face of the earth."*
>
> — FRANCES ANNE KEMBLE, GEORGIA PLANTATION RESIDENT, 1838.

these *crackers* made."

But it was when Florida passed into American hands that Crackers began to populate the state in far greater numbers. In 1821 the new U.S. Territory needed thousands more residents to become a state. To lure more settlers into the undeveloped wilderness, Congress offered land on easy terms to frontiersmen, and people began to pour into Florida from Georgia, Alabama, the Carolinas, and other northern states. These migrants brought with them their ways and beliefs that shaped the early American landscape in

> *"When the horse is harnessed into the cart, they mount his back with a long stick, the walls of the cart serving for stirrups, which bend their knees up to about right angles & 'Off she goes.' Once I saw three cracker women coming to market in this manner on the horse and two sitting in the tail of the cart with their legs hanging out. These are fair samples of the Crackers."*
>
> — NEWTON HENRY, A SOLDIER STATIONED AT FORT HEILMAN DURING THE SECOND SEMINOLE WAR, DESCRIBES IN A LETTER TO CALVIN HENRY DATED NOVEMBER 16, 1839 HOW CRACKERS HITCH HORSES AND COWS TO THEIR CARTS WITH POLES. FROM JAMES DENHAM'S "THE FLORIDA CRACKER BEFORE THE CIVIL WAR AS SEEN THROUGH TRAVELERS' ACCOUNTS," 1994.

Florida. Alternately described as poor whites or Crackers, these settlers were by far the largest cultural group in the state by the first half of the 19th century.[12]

McWhiney explains that conditions throughout the first half of the 19th century were perfect for a large and steady Celtic diffusion into the lower South: " ... Despite the push of westward migration, the Old South remained a thinly populated area of untouched forests and vast grazing lands ... Such a region was ideally suited for the clannish, herding, leisure-loving Celts,

> *"Several long-bearded sallow men with long-napped white hats of ancient pattern, were evidently model specimens of the 'Cracker' race. One of them, a one-eyed fellow, with a black beard down to his waist like ironware, was so truculent-looking that I found myself involuntarily giving him a wide berth, until I fell accidentally into conversation with him, when I discovered him to be a good-natured and mild-spoken person, not without intelligence."*
>
> — CURTIS B. PYLE, A PENNSYLVANIAN TRAVELING THROUGH LOWER GEORGIA, IN A CORRESPONDENCE TO THE *MASONIC MIRROR AND AMERICAN KEYSTONE*, 1840s.

who relished whiskey, gambling, and combat, and who despised hard work, anything English, most government, fences, and any other restraints upon them or their free-ranging livestock."[13]

Some of the best descriptions of Crackers and their lifestyles come from accounts of soldiers who were stationed in the Florida territory and state between the 1830s and the 1860s. Some of these have been chronicled by James Denham in his works.[14] Many Crackers served during the Seminole Indian Wars in volunteer units organized to assist the U.S. Army in protecting rural settlements from Indian attack. There was a pervasive Cracker resentment of the Army, and in turn, commissioned soldiers were not fond of the "Cracker cavalry." "The Volunteers are called Crackers and as a general thing they are a very corrupt set of men," observed Lt. Oliver Howard during the Third Seminole War, "they drink, gamble, and swear and do all manner of discreditable things, and are not withal very good soldiers."[15]

> *"(I had to) sit down to a breakfast with a poor white family ... a man and his wife and four children, belonging to the class called 'crackers' in Georgia ... They are a class of small proprietors, who seem to acquire slovenly habits from dependence upon slaves, of who they can maintain but few."*
>
> — THE NOTED GEOLOGIST SIR CHARLES LYELL RELAYING AN UNANTICIPATED DINING EXPERIENCE WITH A CRACKER FAMILY NEAR DARIEN, GEORGIA, 1845.

In his *The United States of North America*, Achille Murat, exiled nephew of Napoleon, provides a descriptive critique of Crackers traveling through Florida during the Territorial period. While at times slanted, his account of the migrants details their carefree lifestyle: "(The Crackers are) poor citizens usually not very industrious, who not possessing the means of buying lands, live upon those of others, and work them until they are expelled by the proprietors. Their poverty is entirely the fruit of their idle and drunken habits, (and they) pursue this sort of life from choice, from taste, and perhaps, even from habit. For the most part, they have a wife and children,

> *"They are as a class entirely destitute, ignorant, and generally ambitious only for enough to eat regardless of quality to satisfy their hunger. They are governed almost exclusively by the cattle proprietors."*
>
> — A UNION ARMY OFFICER DESCRIBING CRACKER CATTLEHANDS AT MCKAY'S WHARF ON THE PEACE RIVER IN 1865. IN *FLORIDA'S PEACE RIVER FRONTIER*, CANTER BROWN, JR., 1991.

some negroes, and sometimes very numerous flocks. They rarely raise two crops from the same land; on the contrary they quit a district as soon as it becomes peopled."

Murat records meeting a large Cracker family traveling along side a wagon loaded with all their possessions, with some thirty cows and hogs herded in tow: "After questions; Where do you come from? Where are you going? Which are always cordially answered, the head of the family has asked me some details relative to the country, and requested me to direct him to the creek, or the nearest spring. A week after, I have been astonished to see a hut there, a field of cattle, and some poultry; the wife spinning cotton, the husband destroying trees by making a circular incision in them, called a girdle, in short, setting their household goods without making enquiry as to whom the land belonged. Frequently also, I have seen them, after a few days sojourn, abandon their dwelling for the slightest cause, and transport themselves - God Knows where."[16]

The close of the Second Seminole War found many Crackers, particularly those who lived in the north Florida highlands, unable or reluctant to return to the life of a farmer. Many of these settlers were attracted to cattle raising and thousands used the Armed Occupation Act of 1842 to lay claim to vast open range lands and errant herds of cattle farther south. While cattle ranching in Florida spans some four centuries, it was during this period that the cattle industry prospered and the Cracker cowhunter lifestyle emerged, taking on a character which helped shape Florida's distinctive rural cultural landscape.

> "Along these roads at distant intervals were the log-cabin habitations of 'Crackers,' each with its swarm of tow-head, dirty urchins and their slatternly mother. Not to mention the curs and hounds which, when disturbed from their lazy repose by a passing stranger, made the woods resound with their low-bred barking."
>
> — JOHN TIDBALL, 1849, A UNITED STATES OFFICER WHO OBSERVED CRACKER HOMESTEADS WHILE TRAVELING FROM PALATKA TO OCALA. FROM JAMES M. DENHAM'S "CRACKER WOMAN AND THEIR FAMILIES IN NINETEENTH CENTURY FLORIDA," IN FLORIDA'S HERITAGE OF DIVERSITY: ESSAYS IN HONOR OF SAMUEL PROCTOR, 1997.

By the late antebellum period, the term *cracker* was a general designation for non-slaveholding whites of the lower south who represented the lowest rung of the socio-economic ladder.[17] James Stirling noted in 1857 that the Florida society was divided into a wealthy, dominant class and a poor white class of Crackers

"A Florida 'Cracker' In Repose." Pencil sketch by Henry J. Morton, 1867. From St. Augustine, 1867: Drawings by Henry J. Morton, edited and annotated by Thomas Graham. Published by the St. Augustine Historical Society, 1996.

who lived among the pines, raised a few hogs and cows, grew a little patch of corn, and just barely survived.[18] But the editor of the Tallahassee *Florida Sentinel* in 1844 suggests that social stratification in antebellum Florida was more complex and that three classes - planter, overseer and *cracker* or stocktender - were prevalent, indicating the association of many Crackers with cattle raising.[19]

During the Civil War, the Florida cattle ranges were battlegrounds for Confederate drovers and Union patrols. Cattle was so important to the war effort that Crackers were hired to herd and protect both Union and Confederate livestock, with many serving in a special Confederacy detail known as the Cow Cavalry. Others made a good living smuggling cattle and supplies through Union blockades. There is some debate on the political agenda of Crackers during the war and their views on the institution of slavery. Travel accounts suggest that Crackers were mostly anti-Confederate, but it is not clear if they supported the Union campaign.[20] After the war, the debt-ridden state sold off much of the land that Crackers had used for grazing cattle, sending hundreds of landless stockraisers back to an agricultural-based way of life, although a number of well-established cattlemen continued to prosper. Many Florida cowmen of this period were drifting veterans of the Civil War or fugitives seeking sanctuary. Some even amassed their herds by stealing cattle from the Seminole Indians.

Canter Brown, Jr. offers this perspective on the difference between Peace River area stockmen who arrived just prior to the Civil War and post-war Cracker migrants: "While most earlier settlers were involved to a greater or lessor extent in the cattle business, the newcomers were mostly farmers, many of them poor. Although the war had reduced most of the earlier settlers to modest economic circumstances, that was not true of the cattlemen. Those men were growing wealthy, and their interests were clear and distinct from those of the newcomers."[21]

In the tide of immigration that followed the Civil War, a whole new population of settlers found their way into the state. These new Florida Crackers were mostly an impoverished and poorly educated people who were driven out of their homelands by the adversities of war and lured to the wilds of Florida by rumored opportunity. They found much of the former and little of the latter, but were tenacious enough to establish themselves firmly in rural areas throughout Florida. Throughout the 20th century, they came with little, not knowing their destinations, drifting into the state in carts and wagons, down dusty dirt roads, driving what little livestock they had with the crack of the whip. The new migrants caused discord in some areas, but were assimilated into existing Cracker settlements in other parts. Most sought out the remote backwoods of Florida to settle in isolation. Their strong country backgrounds and their experience with hardship allowed them to endure until they were firmly rooted in their sometimes hostile, backwoods environment. From this stock, rural peoples of Florida emerged on better ground.

> "(Crackers are) soft-voiced, easy-going, childlike kind of folk, quick to anger, vindictive when their rage is protracted and becomes a feud; and generous and noble in their rough hospitality. But they live the most undesirable of lives, and surrounded by every facility for a luxurious existence, subsist on 'hog and hominy,' and drink the meanest whiskey."
>
> — EDWARD KING, *THE GREAT SOUTH*, 1875.

The Victorian perception of this second wave of immigrants was mostly a disparaging one. In the late 19th century, Crackers were easy fodder for writers traveling through the state looking for colorful anecdotes for a northern reading public. The misunderstood Florida backwoods settlers were caricatured in cartoons and parodied in print across America. One of the most patronizing descriptions of Crackers of this period was written by George M. Barbour, a puritan New Englander who toured Florida in 1882: "The entire

The Cracker way of life has been misunderstood for centuries. Throughout the 1800s, the backwoods settlers were parodied in print as drunken, unruly Southerners who had a great aversion to work and material prosperity. This image captures the "red-nosed, tobacco-drizzling, whiskey-perfumed Cracker" stereotype described in De Forest's post-Civil War Miss Ravenel. *From* Harper's New Monthly Magazine, *1861, p. 607.*

trip that day was through an unsettled region, the only human beings living anywhere along the road being four or five families of Florida natives, the genuine, unadulterated 'cracker' - the clay-eating, gaunt, pale, tallowy, leather-skinned sort - stupid, stolid, staring eyes, dead and lusterless; unkempt hair, generally tow-colored; and such a shiftless, slouching manner! Simply white savages - or living white mummies would, perhaps, better indicate their dead-alive looks and actions. Stupid and shiftless, yet sly and vindictive, they are a block in the pathway of civilization, settlement, and enterprise wherever they exist."

> *"The Cracker may be defined as the poor man that prefers ease to hardship, content with little, jealous of intrusion into his unkempt life, shrewd, narrow, uncouth, unlettered, homely, conservative."*
>
> — JAMES WOOD DAVIDSON, 1888.

In 1875, Florida traveler Sidney Lanier offered this near-poetic once-over of a Cracker settler on the Ocklawaha River, describing his subject in great detail, right down to the hair on his head: "He is a slim native, and there is not bone enough in his whole body to make the left leg of a good English coal-heaver: moreover, he does not seem to have the least idea that a man needs grooming. He is disheveled and wry-trussed to the last degree; his poor weasel jaws nearly touch their inner sides as they suck at the acrid ashes in his dreadful pipe; and

"Cracker with Ox Team near Stuart, Florida." Covered wagons were used by immigrants well into the 20th century as shown by this c. 1915 photograph. Photograph, Florida State Archives.

there is no single filament of either his hair or his beard that does not look sourly, and at wild angles, upon its neighbor filament. His eyes are viscidly unquiet; his nose is merely dreariness come to a point; the corners of his mouth are pendulous with that sort of suffering which does not involve any heroism, such as being out of tobacco, waiting for the corn bread to get cooked, and the like.[22] Other writers were more sympathetic, like Samuel Fairbanks who in 1877 offered this defense of the settlers: "the Florida cracker is an independent, self-supporting citizen ... a quiet, good citizen who develops the country to some purpose by honest toil."[23]

> "Keen-eyed Yankee visitors had already written about the people who made up the almost unseen background of the state, calling them 'natives' or 'Crackers,' lank whiskered men, tobacco stained, with the marks of malaria on them; thin bony wives, and sallow, white-headed children. They had retreated after the war into deeper wilderness, in the immemorial rugged frontier life of log cabin and clearing, hunting and fishing. They were seen driving rickety oxcarts along pine woods roads, or coming in barefooted to boat landing stores to trade skins or deer meat for chewing tobacco, snuff, bacon, calico, powder. Sometimes they worked at logging or sawmilling. They had taken the place of the almost vanished Indian in the remote country where they kept alive the legends, the ballads, the tunes, the customs of their Georgian, Carolinian, Scotch-Irish, Irish, English, or even German ancestry. They were, as they had been, proud, secretive, unlettered, suspicious, enduring as time. They had taken the land for their own and had held it, making it American. It would be a long time before anyone noticed them more closely."
>
> — MARJORY STONEMAN DOUGLAS IN HER *FLORIDA: THE LONG FRONTIER*, 1967, DESCRIBES THE CRACKER STATE OF AFFAIRS IN SOUTH FLORIDA, JUST AFTER THE CIVIL WAR.

Because they were of different cultural backgrounds, visitors throughout the history of Florida found the Cracker peoples to be unusual. Fascinated with their odd customs and mannerisms, Northern travelers took notice of and remarked upon even the most common of Cracker behaviors. While at times deprecating, these accounts provide historians with a rare and important glimpse into the lives of rural Cracker settlers who seldom recorded their own history.

SUGGESTED READING

James M. Denham, "The Florida Cracker Before the Civil War as Seen Through Travelers' Accounts." *Florida Historical Quarterly* 72 (4), 1994.

James M. Denham, "Cracker Woman and Their Families in Nineteenth Century Florida," In *Florida's Heritage of Diversity: Essays in Honor of Samuel Proctor*. Mark I. Greenberg, William Warren Rogers, and Canter Brown, Jr., editors. Tallahassee: Sentry Press, 1997.

James M. Denham, "Cracker Times and Pioneer Lives, The Florida Reminiscences of George Gillett Keen and Sarah Pamela Williams." Book in preparation.

James E. Lewis, "Cracker - Spanish Florida Style." *Florida Historical Quarterly* 63, 1984, 186.

NOTES

1. Charles Reagan Wilson and William Ferris, editors, "Crackers," *Encyclopedia of Southern Culture* (1989), p. 1132.

2. Hugh Rawson, *Wicked Words*, 1989, 99. Henry Laurens in *Bernard Bailyn's Voyagers to the West: A Passage in the Peopling of America on the Eve of the Revolution*. New York: Alfred A. Knopf, 1986, p. 449.

3. Grady McWhiney, *Cracker Culture, Celtic Ways in the Old South*. Tuscaloosa and London: University of Alabama Press, 1988, p. 8.

4. *The Oxford English Dictionary*, Second Edition. Oxford: Clarendon Press, 1989, p. 1099.

5. Draper, *King's Mountain*, 1801, p. 70.

6. Daniel Schafer, "Overview of Eastern Florida Agricultural Themes, 1763 - 1850." Paper presented at the Northeastern Florida Plantation Symposium, Daytona Beach, March 22, 1997.

7. Governor Wright, letter of December, 1771, in Delma E. Presley, "The Crackers of Georgia." *The Georgia Historical Quarterly* 60 (2), 1976.

8. Delma E. Presley, "The Crackers of Georgia," 1976, p. 103.

9. James E. Lewis, "Cracker - Spanish Florida Style." *Florida Historical Quarterly* 63, 1984, p. 186.

10. Letter from Luis de las Casas to Conde del Campo de Alange, August 14, 1790, translated by James E. Lewis, "Cracker - Spanish Florida Style," p. 188.

11. Manuel de Zespedes letter, 1790, translated by James E. Lewis, "Cracker - Spanish Florida Style," p. 191.

12. James M. Denham, "The Florida Cracker Before the Civil War as Seen Through Travelers' Accounts." *Florida Historical Quarterly* 72 (4), 1994, p. 454.

13. Grady McWhiney, *Cracker Culture, Celtic Ways in the Old South*. Tuscaloosa and London: University of Alabama Press, 1988, p. 8.

14. James M. Denham, "The Florida Cracker Before the Civil War as Seen Through Travelers' Accounts." *Florida Historical Quarterly* 72, 1994; "Some Prefer the Seminoles: Violence Among Soldiers and Settlers in the Second Seminole War, 1835 - 1842," *Florida Historical Quarterly* 70, 1991; "Cracker Woman and Their Families in Nineteenth Century Florida," in, *Florida's Heritage of Diversity: Essays in Honor of Samuel Proctor*. Mark I. Greenberg, William Warren Rogers, and Canter Brown, Jr., editors. Tallahassee: Sentry Press, 1997.

15. Canter Brown, Jr., *Florida's Peace River Frontier*. Orlando: University of Central Florida Press, 1991, p. 109.

16. Achille Murat, *The United States of North America* (London, 1833), pp. 51 - 54.

17. Delma E. Presley, *"The Crackers of Georgia,"* 1976, p. 106.

18. James Stirling, 1857, in Benjamin F. Rogers, "Florida Seen Through the Eyes of Nineteenth Century Travellers." *Florida Historical Quarterly* 34, no. 2 (October 1955), p. 186.

19. In Dodd, "Florida in 1845: Statistics, economic life, and social life," *Florida Historical Quarterly* XVIV, July 1945, p. 10.

20. James M. Denham, "The Florida Cracker Before the Civil War as Seen Through Travelers' Accounts." 1994, p. 468.

21. Canter Brown, Jr. *Florida's Peace River Frontier*, 1991, p. 196.

22. Sidney Lanier, *Florida: Its Scenery, Climate and History*. Philadelphia, 1875; reprint ed., Bicentennial Floridiana Facsimile Series, Gainesville: University of Florida Press, 1973, pp. 18 - 19.

23. Samuel Fairbanks, "The Florida Cracker," *The Semi-Tropical: A Monthly Journal Devoted To Southern Agriculture, Horticulture, and To Immigration*, September 1877, p. 526.

A Cracker child. From The Great South *by Edward King, 1875.*

The Cracker Culture

"Who, or what, these 'crackers' are, from whom descended, of what nationality, or what becomes of them, is one among the many unsolved mysteries in this state."
— GEORGE M. BARBOUR, A NEW ENGLANDER
WHO TRAVELED TO FLORIDA IN 1882.

Of the many rich themes in Florida history, the story of the Cracker is perhaps the most colorful and most endearing to visitors and residents. Entrenched in Florida folklore, romanticized in the literature, and celebrated year after year in festivals throughout the state, the Florida Cracker culture nonetheless remains poorly understood.

Theories abound on when the Cracker culture emerged, but by the late 18th century the term *cracker* commonly was used to describe a widespread population of white settlers in the South - not the age-old character trait it originally implied. Many of these settlers were of Celtic stock, and some scholars have noted how the Cracker lifestyle closely resembles the traditional Celtic culture, one which was very different from that of Anglo-Saxon New England colonists of the time. Like the clans of the Highland Scots and the fiefdoms of the Irish, Florida Crackers were expert herdsmen with solid kinship ties.

Grady McWhiney's *Cracker Culture: Celtic Ways in the Old South* (1988) describes how the South was settled and dominated numerically during the antebellum period by immigrants from the Celtic regions of the British Isles, including Scotland, Ireland, Wales, and Cornwall, and the English uplands: "By the time of the American Revolution there were Celts throughout the South, but the greatest concentration of them was in the backcountry from Pennsylvania to Georgia. Along that frontier they outnumbered all other settlers ..."[1] The idea of the Celtic origins of the early white Southerner class is perhaps the most thoroughly examined, albeit controversial, theories on the emergence of the Cracker culture. But clearly, these Celtic settlers had a profound impact on the Southern way of life during the antebellum, an influence Forrest McDonald and McWhiney sum up nicely: "The Celts who settled in the South brought with them their non-English ways - including a pastoral economy based on open-range herding, a leisurely lifestyle and a distaste for hard work, rural values that stressed wasteful hospitality and outdoor sports, the reckless indulgence in food and drink, a touchy and romantic sense of honor, and a strong tendency toward lawlessness and the settlement of disagreements by violent means - and they readily imposed these traditions upon their neighbors. Only a few settlers in the antebellum South, such as determined Yankees and isolated Germans as well as the enslaved Africans, managed to avoid acculturation into the prevailing Celtic culture patterns."[2] McWhiney suggests that the fundamental and lasting division between the North and the South began in colonial America when these Irish and Scottish peoples instilled their traditional customs and beliefs in the Old South.[3]

Author Gloria Jahoda is uncertain of this pervasive Celtic heritage, at least in west Florida, and for different reasons: "It is in the western panhandle that the cracker is racially and culturally the least diluted. He is tall and rangy, with the angular bones of the Scotch-Irish and blue eyes the Saxons and Celts acquired more than a thousand years ago when Vikings raided their villages. 'A hot Scotland!' one of my friends once exclaimed after her first day in the panhandle. 'They're all so intense, so Calvinistic, so clan-loyal and proud.' But I had my reservations about her verdict then, and I still have. The Scotch in Scotland today are not noted for anything approaching talkative southern hospitality. The crackers, in my experience, are."[4]

In examining the ethnicity of Southerners topically rather than chronologically, McWhiney emphasizes culture as the principal determinant in the development of Crackers. In this framework, it is likely that settlers with ethnic backgrounds other than Celtic were part of the same Cracker culture, something McWhiney acknowledges in his work: "Such family histories exist, but there simply are not enough of them to prove that most of the people who settled the Old South were of Celtic descent."[5] Of the many Cracker Floridians interviewed for the current study, three-quarters of them claimed at least some Celtic heritage. But many have diverse ethnic backgrounds with ancestors from England, Germany, Russia, the Netherlands, and Spain, among other places. One of the most noted Cracker homesteads in Moultrie, Florida was settled in the late 19th century by a Minorcan family, the Pellicers, whose antecedents had earlier adopted the Cracker way of life, possibly as early as 1777 when Minorcan colonists were resettled in the St. Augustine area by British Governor Patrick Tonyn from the failed colony of New Smyrna.[6] Near Jacksonville, there

Pellicer's Log Cabin in Moultrie, Florida. Photograph taken by F. A. Meyer in 1884; printed from the original glass plate negative by Ken Barrett, Jr. Meyer's photograph was reproduced as a drawing by his son E. A. Meyer in Pen Drawings of St. Augustine and Other Views of Florida, *1940. The work was entitled, "A Florida Log House at Moultrie, Five Miles below St. Augustine, Fla." Photograph and drawing from the collection of The St. Augustine Historical Society.*

"Cracker" settlers, possibly Minorcan, on their way to market in St. Augustine, Florida, March 20, 1893. Behind the woman seated in the donkey-drawn cart is a basket of chickens. From the collection of the St. Augustine Historical Society.

is a long-established community of Crackers of Lebanese-Syrian ancestry. And there is much evidence of African Americans and Native Americans living the Cracker way. John Dederer suggests that "the tribal Celtic-Southerner's culture and folk traits were so compatible with those of the Africans that it took little adaptation for slaves to fit Celtic characteristics around their African practices."[7] F. R. Swift's recounting of a horse-riding accident in the late 19th century includes a reference to a "Cracker" African-American: "I knew the best thing for him was a doctor, and as the nearest one was at Ocala, six miles away, I told them to saddle my favorite horse and I would go.

> *"(The Crackers) are tall, sturdy, bold, addicted to drinking, and habituated to interlarding their words with terrible curses. Accustomed to living alone in the woods, they have adopted the habits of savages with who they are in constant contact; at every moment their conversation is interrupted with war cries. They leap about and howl, and make no effort to restrain their passions."*
>
> — COMTE DE CASTELNAU,
> *ESSAY ON MIDDLE FLORIDA, 1837 - 1838.*

But Brown, the Captain's valet and bodyguard, absolutely refused to allow any of the colored crackers to saddle him."[8]

McWhiney notes that many of the Indians of the Old South practiced lifestyles similar to those of their Celtic neighbors.[9] Manuel de Zespedes in 1790 makes reference to these "crackerized" Native Americans in Florida: "The Americans take advantage of the ignorance of the savage and his affection for the English by pretending to be from Great Britain. This makes it easier for them to live among the savages. Once there, Americans slowly but surely wean away the loyalty that Indian *crackers* of British descent have for us." In the same letter Zespedes recognizes a degree of mutual acculturation: "In the war between England and her colonies, the Indians in general and many *crackers* in particular followed the loyalist side. As a result, the two developed a strong bond for one another. Since the loyalist *crackers* were so closely tied to the royalist and losing side in the conflict, they found themselves pursued and persecuted by their enemies and were forced to take refuge in this Florida and with the Creeks." This entry also identifies an

> *"Alternately disparaged, patronized, and ignored, these people have never received what every group is entitled to - a sympathetic look into their history that seeks to understand them on their own terms."*
>
> — JAMES M. DENHAM, "THE FLORIDA CRACKER BEFORE THE CIVIL WAR AS SEEN THROUGH TRAVELERS' ACCOUNTS." *FLORIDA HISTORICAL QUARTERLY*, 1994.

Some African-Americans in Florida adopted the Cracker way of life. Photograph c. 1890s. Collection of the author.

atypical brand of Cracker that was loyal to the Crown.

And at least one Frenchman tried, albeit in vain, to live for himself the Florida Cracker way of life. In 1824, Achille Murat, Crown Prince of Naples, nephew of Napoleon, and relative by marriage of George Washington, arrived in St. Augustine, and quickly gained a reputation for his peculiar behavior, such as beating the Florida heat and insects by lowering himself in a chair into the Matanzas River with mosquito netting on his head. Murat was reluctant to change clothes, had an aversion to water, and often boasted that when he donned a new pair of boots, they would be worn until they fell off. But perhaps his most curious habit, as one of his neighbors once noted, was his obsession with "the eatability of the whole animal tribe." Expanding on the culinary know-how of his Cracker neighbors, and into areas which had long been tested and rejected by even Cracker standards, Murat made a regular diet of such

unusual fare as baked turkey buzzard, boiled owl, roasted crow, stewed alligator, lizards and rattlesnakes.[10]

Whether or not all Crackers were of Celtic heritage, it is evident that they were culturally distinct from Northern pioneer groups, and that collectively these backwoods settlers and stockmen shared similar customs, habits, and material traits - a way of life that could only be described as a culture - the Cracker culture. By this definition, *cracker* does not signify an economic condition, but a patterned lifestyle, although poverty, at least during some periods of Florida history, undoubtedly helped shape the culture.

A portrait of Prince Achille Murat in his 40s c. 1845. Artist unknown. Florida State Archives.

The Murat House, St. Augustine, Florida. E. A. Meyer in his tourist folio, From Supplement to Pen Drawings of St. Augustine and Other Views of Florida, by E. A. Meyer, 1946. From the collection of the St. Augustine Historical Society.

Photograph of Fred Harding and Jesse Dreggors in a lighter moment at their hunt camp on the St. Johns River, c. 1900. Crackers adapted well to the diverse environments of Florida. Photograph from the collection of Bill Dreggors, DeLand.

Defining Cracker's simply as "Southerners," "white settlers," or "pioneers" ignores the distinctiveness of Cracker culture. Take for example Delma E. Presley's attempt at boiling down the Cracker culture to two words: "A proper definition of the term "Cracker" should take into account both cultural and linguistic information. One noun summarizes his cultural history: *pioneer*. One adjective expresses his image in English usage as early as the eighteenth century: *proud*. Thus we should define Georgia's Cracker simply as a *proud pioneer*."[11] *Cracker* and *pioneer* should not be used interchangeably as many Southern "pioneers" did not practice a way of life which characterizes the Cracker existence. If succinctness becomes necessary, a more fitting definition of a Cracker is "a self-sufficient inhabitant who scratches his/her living from the soil or from raising livestock," James Denham's poignant

> *"In the winter we lives on yankees, and in the summer on catfish."*
> — ANONYMOUS FLORIDA CRACKER,
> EARLY 20TH CENTURY.
> STETSON KENNEDY FILES, FLORIDA STATE ARCHIVES.

description of a Southern "plain folk" culture which includes a middle class, illustrating that Crackers were more than just poor whites.[12]

Self-sufficiency was a signature characteristic of Crackers. The tenacity and self-reliance of these 19th century and early 20th century pioneers helped them adapt to and settle the diverse environs of Florida, some considered largely uninhabitable. While Crackers were bound by similar cultural traits, the different environmental regions they occupied offered natural resources unique to those areas, and these environs required specialized means of settlement and forms of technologies to ensure survival. From that which was offered by the land, Crackers carved out an existence highly adaptive to the environment in which they lived, much like the Native Americans who preceded them.

Some groups of Crackers settled the southwest coast of Florida, surviving by, among other things, fishing, growing sugar cane, or sometimes collecting bird plumes, while others in the north-central highland scrub relied on hog-raising, plot-gardening and sometimes wild game hunting. Coastal Crackers harvested shellfish and riverdwellers on the St. Johns catfished and hunted alligators for hides. Still others raised livestock or worked as cowhunters for cattle ranches. Regionally, subcultures emerged throughout Florida, from the lower Appalachian foothills to the Keys. Clearly, subsistence adaptation was a major determinant of regional cultural variability.

> *"Settlers thus opening up the lower east and west coasts, varied in their backgrounds, beliefs and traditions, were alike and united in the courage and resourcefulness they brought to their hard, primitive lives. They battled similar plagues of mosquitos, sand flies and blood-sucking deer flies with smudge fires under the windows of their log houses or even inside their windowless, dirt-floored palmetto shacks. Beds were often bunks. Palmetto hats were draped with mosquito net. Rattlesnakes slid over doorless sills. Wildcats and alligators stole chickens, panthers and wolves killed heifers and pigs, and black bears robbed gardens everywhere.*
>
> *West coast woman cooked outside on 'scaffold' stoves,' log bins roofed, and floored with sand, while east coast woman built their fires on the ground. West coast mattresses were of ancestral feathers or live oak moss. On the east coast they were stuffed with palmetto fronds, shredded with steel forks. All men wore butternut or blue homespun jeans; all women, limp calicoes and sunbonnets."*
>
> — MARJORY STONEMAN DOUGLAS IN HER *FLORIDA: THE LONG FRONTIER*, 1967, OFFERS THIS INSIGHT ON THE LATE 19TH CENTURY CULTURAL DIFFERENCES OF SOUTHWEST AND SOUTHEAST FLORIDA CRACKER SETTLERS, AND THE SIMILARITIES OF THEIR DIFFICULT EXISTENCE.

Historical and ethnographic studies of these regional adaptations should

An early 20th century Cracker family living off the land in South Florida. Florida State Archives.

shed great light on the differences and similarities of all Cracker subcultures in Florida - the varying means of coping with diverse environments, but, most important, the cultural universals which bind all Cracker peoples. To date, only a few such studies have been undertaken, including folklorists Bucuvalas, Bulger, and Kennedy's ethnography of South Florida Crackers, a culmination of state-sponsored fieldwork and research.[13] It is a concise work, but one which is packed with information, and it should serve nicely as a model for subsequent studies of other Cracker subcultures in Florida.

Their study captures well the regional Cracker adaptation of coastal southern Florida: "Beginning as hunters of plumes and pelts, then establishing vast open-range ranches, year-round produce or citrus farms, and lucrative fishing businesses, South Florida Crackers tamed the tropics and brought their unique culture into what would become a truly multicultural region." Ranching, farming, fishing, transportation, architecture, language, oral lore, and even underground occupations are examined by the authors as constructs of the Cracker culture of this region. Another excellent ethnographic study of a coastal Cracker fishing group is Robert F. Edic's *Fisherfolk of Charlotte Harbor*, Florida (1996).

A rich and unforgettable image of 19th century Cracker life along the southwest coast of Florida is detailed in a novel by Peter Matthiessen, *Killing*

"An Indian Stock-Drover." From **The Great South** *by Edward King, 1875, p. 201. In the 19th century, many Native Americans of the South practiced lifestyles similar to their Cracker neighbors.*

Mister Watson (1991). Although a work of fiction, Matthiessen's meticulous research, based largely on historical and oral accounts, is evident throughout the book. It is brilliantly written and very convincing, offering an intricate and seemingly firsthand look at early Cracker settlement and existence in the remote Ten Thousand Island region.

A similar scenario of the interior scrub Cracker subculture can be reconstructed based on early written accounts of these hinterland settlements and people, some of which are explored in the next chapter. Patrick Smith drew largely upon these historical and oral accounts, as well as personal experience, for his fictional, *A Land Remembered*. Here, he depicts the difficult and challenging life of Cracker settler of the remote Florida interior during Civil War times: "... Because his homestead was so isolated, he knew little of what was happening. Occasionally a stranger would drift by and give him the news. He would also hear of the war when he made trips to a small settlement on the St. Johns River to trade animal hides for supplies.

The first two years in Florida had been a time of near starvation. He cleared a garden and planted his precious seeds, but the poor sandy soil offered little in return. And the wild animals were a constant problem when plants did break through into the sunlight. Deer, turkey, and hogs were plentiful in the woods, but

Wild turkey and other game were an important source of food for scrub Crackers. The birds were abundant, but required expensive shotgun shells to hunt.

shells were so hard to come by that he could kill only when it was an absolute necessity to survive. Also during the first year, panthers killed the guinea cow and left only a pile of shattered bones.

During this time they lived in a lean-to

made of pine limbs and palmetto thatch. There was nothing to ward off the summer mosquitoes and the roaming rattlesnakes and the rain and the biting winter cold. Emma feared for the safety of the baby, and they finally made a crude hammock so that she could at least keep him off the ground.

In the second year, Tobias started building the house, cutting the logs in a nearby hammock and dragging them to the site with the oxen, shaping the logs and lumber by hand, building a wall one torturous foot at a time. The roof was of cypress shingles, and devoting what time he could to produce them, he made twenty-five each day. It took more than five hundred to build the roof. More than a year of sweat and pain went into the rugged structure before it was complete enough for them to move inside. Yet ahead of him was the task of building beds and tables and chairs and completing the mud and stone fireplace ...

He also found that nothing would grow on pine ridges but

A temporary Cracker homestead in a stand of cabbage palms on a swamp margin. From Florida Fancies *by F. R. Swift, 1903, p. 68.*

An early hand-fashioned Cracker log home near Moultrie, Florida. This mid-19th century house, now gone, was documented in E. A. Meyer's Supplement to Pen Drawings of St. Augustine and Other Views of Florida *(1946) as a drawing entitled "An Abandoned Shack in Florida." The image was originally produced as a photograph by his father F. A. Meyer in the 1880s. From the collection of the St. Augustine Historical Society.*

many food plants would survive in hammock ground, and after the second year he moved his garden away from the house area and into a nearby hammock.

A man in the St. Johns settlement told him that twenty miles to the west there was a herd of wild cows. They were too wild for anyone to ever catch without dogs and horses, but in one grazing area they had littered the ground with manure. Tobias went there with his wagon and brought back a load of manure for the garden, and each spring he would return for another load of the life-giving fertilizer."[14]

"But one thing about Crackers is that we can always perform beneath your lowest expectations. And we have our moments when we can display great nobility."

— JOURNALIST JOHN CARTER FROM HIS SUNDAY PUNCH COLUMN, "CONNOTATION OF 'CRACKER' HOLDS STRONG." *THE DAYTONA BEACH NEWS-JOURNAL*, SEPTEMBER 7, 1997.

A general defining trait of the early Cracker culture in Florida is that material possessions meant little to these self-reliant settlers. To Crackers everywhere in the state, personal independence and a restraint-free life were far

Belle Glade family, c. 1939. To many Crackers, independence and unrestricted living were more important than material prosperity, and these traits shaped a large segment of the culture. Photograph, Florida State Archives.

more important than material prosperity or work - a behavior often viewed as lazy and shiftless by outsiders who did not understand the Cracker way of life. What few goods Crackers owned were usually home-made and rarely "store-boughten," for they seldom had the money to buy things. Typically, Cracker materials like cloth, tools and cooking pots were used everyday until they wore out, which explains why little early Cracker material culture has survived today for study.

Suggested Reading

Tina Bucuvalas, Peggy A. Bulger, and Stetson Kennedy, "The Crackers." In *South Florida Folklife*. Jackson: University Press of Mississippi, 1994, pp. 37 - 63.

Grady McWhiney, *Cracker Culture, Celtic Ways in the Old South*. Tuscaloosa and London: University of Alabama Press, 1988.

Peter Matthiessen, *Killing Mister Watson*. New York: Vintage, 1991.

Notes

1. Grady McWhiney, *Cracker Culture, Celtic Ways in the Old South*. Tuscaloosa and London: University of Alabama Press, 1988.

2. Forrest McDonald and Grady McWhiney, "Celtic South," *Encyclopedia of Southern Culture*, 1989, pp. 1131 - 1132.

3. McWhiney, *Cracker Culture*, xiii.

4. Gloria Jahoda, *The Other Florida*. New York: Charles Scribner's Sons, 1967, p. 55.

5. McWhiney, *Cracker Culture*, 15.

6. Conversation with Charles A. Tingley, Reference Librarian with the St. Augustine Historical Society Library, March 1997.

7. John Morgan Dederer, "Afro-Southern and Celtic-Southern Cultural Adaptation in the Old South," manuscript on file, Florida State Archives.

8. F. R. Swift, *Florida Fancies*. New York and London: G.P. Putnam's Sons, 1903, p. 29.

9. McWhiney, *Cracker Culture*, p. 21.

10. Dana Ste.Claire, "Murat: A Prince and his Palace in St. Augustine," *Florida History Notebook, Arts & Sciences Magazine*, winter 1991; A. J. Hanna, *A Prince in their Midst: The Adventurous Life of Achille Murat on the American Frontier*. Norman: University of Oklahoma Press, 1946.

11. Delma E. Presley, "The Crackers of Georgia." *The Georgia Historical Quarterly* 60 (2), 1976, p. 114.

12. James M. Denham, "Cracker Woman and Their Families in Nineteenth Century Florida," In, *Florida's Heritage of Diversity: Essays in Honor of Samuel Proctor*. Mark I. Greenberg, William Warren Rogers, and Canter Brown, Jr., editors. Tallahassee: Sentry Press, 1997.

13. Peggy A. Bulger, and Stetson Kennedy, "The Crackers." In, *South Florida Folklife*. By Tina Bucuvalas, Jackson: University Press of Mississippi, 1994, pp. 37 - 63.

14. Patrick D. Smith, *A Land Remembered*. Sarasota: Pineapple Press, 1984, pp. 13 - 15.

Young Crackers on a split rail fence. From The Great South *by Edward King, 1875, p. 730.*

Saw-Toothed Scrub:
Cracker Life in the Backwoods

"Once we met an old man - originally white, but sunburnt to more than mulatto brown, in a faded blue flannel shirt, with no coat, but in the stead thereof a blanket - (in urgent need of being sent to the laundry) - pinned round his shoulders with a skewer, a hugh straw hat with half the brim divorced from the crown, an ancient-fashioned gun in one hand, and in the other the spoils of the chase, a coon and two grey squirrels, which he was offering for sale."

— Iza Duffus Hardy, *Oranges and Alligators*, 1887.

Over the years the Cracker lifestyle has been softened in literary works, sometimes shrouding just how difficult the Cracker existence was. It is easy to forget that early Florida settlers had to make do without many conveniences we take for granted today. Luxuries like air-conditioners, refrigerators, automobiles, electric can openers, or even cans for that matter, were far beyond the imagination of these original homesteaders. Eighteenth century through early 20th century life in Florida backwoods was nothing short of demanding. Back then, Crackers spent most of their day providing their families with food and what few other necessities were required to survive.

Early on, Cracker migrants spent a great deal of time traveling from one place to another, rarely settling down. The nomadic and elusive nature of Crackers has been documented many times throughout Florida history, beginning in 1766 when a Colonial official described Crackers as "lawless rascals ... who often change their abode."[1] The Comte de Castelnau, a French naturalist traveling in Florida in 1838, noted the same: "They put all that they own in their wagons and go through the woods hunting for a new dwelling sometimes a hundred leagues from the former one. [They] do not own their land ... but settle in the first place that they find vacant, without being concerned about the name of the owner, who, if he comes to assert his authority, does not receive more response than a bullet from a rifle."[2] Even later, their tendency for mobility is described

Cracker migrants near covered wagon, northern Florida c. 1895. This photograph offers a rare look at Cracker settlers migrating into North Florida. It is unlikely that the father of this family was the photographer, as transient Crackers seldom owned expensive items like cameras. He was probably out hunting for that evening's dinner when an anonymous photographer wandered by to capture this important image. The photograph shows a Cracker family with their hound preparing for an overnight stay in the pine flatwoods of Florida, probably during the winter months judging from the clothing. Supplies and personal items are seen as well, including from left to right a wooden staved water bucket (hanging from the homemade wagon tongue), a stoneware jug for carrying water, a graniteware pan, a kerosene lantern (also hanging from the tongue), an overstuffed chest of cloths, what appears to be a tarp assembly under the wagon, and a wooden wash tub. Out of the camera's range is the mule or ox, or possibly a team of oxen, which pulled the covered wagon. Photograph, Florida State Archives.

"Tired by a long days journey; they wanted to cross (the Chattahoochee River) and called loudly for the boatman to go and get them; the latter lying carelessly in his ferry boat heard them for an hour but did not condescend to even answer them; finally, at my urging he decided to do his duty, but having been rebuked rather keenly by the travelers, he coolly seized a pistol and fired point blank at one of them who miraculously was not hit."

— COMTE DE CASTELNAU IN HIS *ESSAY ON MIDDLE FLORIDA, 1837 - 1838*, COMMENTS ON THE UNPREDICTABLE TEMPERAMENT OF A CRACKER FERRY OPERATOR.

by Frank Hatheway, a dry goods store clerk who witnessed the migration of Crackers into east Florida in 1846. When he asked a Cracker family where they were headed, one replied that "they had no specific destination, but would 'sit down' at the first place that pleased them."[3]

Throughout the 1800s, many groups of Crackers followed cattle herds and cowmen across Florida for survival and protection, as the cowhunter camps offered refuge from hostile Indians. The Cracker migrants were given any leftover food from a cattle butchering or game kill. In return, the vagabond settlers helped out with the daily cattle-tending chores.

In the 19th century and early 20th century, Cracker settlers in covered wagons and homemade carts migrated by the thousands into Florida down dusty rural roads and through open stands of pine forests. Covered wagons often provided the only shelter for wandering Cracker families. Supplies were carried in the wagon along with the very young and elderly. Other family members usually walked or rode horses along side.

In the 19th century, Cracker migrants by the thousands drifted into Florida down dusty rural roads in covered wagons or homemade ox and mule carts. What little livestock they had was driven with the crack of the whip.

Wagon Works

Covered wagons in the 19th century and the early 20th century were a principal form of transportation for Americans, especially for those who traveled great distances across the continent. They were the automobiles of their day, and like cars, were available in different makes and models. Crackers learned early on how to convert their handmade ox carts and supply wagons into cross-country vehicles simply by bending a few green willow branches into an arched frame on a wagon and covering it with canvas or cloth. But at another level, manufactured wagons were big business with a lengthy history as John Latham points out. Latham, one of just a handful of historic wagon experts in the nation, explains that the craft was mostly an English trade which was brought to the New World as early as the 16th century. The American version of the covered wagon known best today was designed during the 17th and 18th centuries. Later, wagon builders modified their design to create a vehicle

Covered wagon, c. 1900, made by the John Deere Company, Moline, Illinois. From the collection of John and Cameron Latham, Jenny's Mule Ranch. Large, manufactured wagons like this John Deere were expensive models that settlers could rarely afford. This was one of the last models produced by John Deere. Around the turn of the century, the company dropped their wagon line and concentrated on the production of farm machinery. Photograph by Roger Simms, 1997.

John and Cameron Latham at their famous Jenny's Mule Ranch store off Old Pioneer Trail in Samsula, Florida. The Latham's keep an impressive collection of early American wagons and carriages at the Ranch. John, a head mule skinner and wagon master drove his covered supply wagon and team across the state during the Sesquicentennial Great Florida Cattle Drive in 1995. He has also worked with a number of motion picture productions supplying wagons, training drivers, and appearing as an extra. Photograph courtesy of Jenny's Mule Ranch.

which could move freight and families to new frontiers. Of interest is that wagons made east of the Mississippi were smaller because of the congestion and narrow roads of East Coast cities. West of the river, wagons like the Conestoga were made larger and heavier to endure the long journeys westward.

Although there were many small wagon manufacturing plants in the eastern United States during the 19th century, the largest companies in the nation were Owensboro in Kentucky and John Deere of Moline, Illinois. The Owensboro Wagon Company plant was ten city blocks long, three city blocks wide, and four stories high. Here, a number of wagon models were produced including the standard one- and two-ton wagons, and a mammoth ten-ton military supply vehicle. The wagons were assembled with manufactured parts which could be purchased individually. Altogether, a complete wagon with a cover and seat would cost about $115.00 in the late 19th century. The Owensboro Company manufactured wagons right up through the late 1940s. They closed after Ford trucks and other motorized vehicles and farm equipment became popular during this time.

At night, everyone would sleep under a tarp pulled from the side of the wagon, if one was available. Water was carried in large canteens mounted to the outside of the wagon and supplies were hung anywhere there was room. For stopping, a large pole next to the driver's seat applied brakes to the wheels.

When a Cracker finally settled in one place, it was typically done in the middle of nowhere, as they were accustomed to living alone or in a sparse scattering of Cracker families. On isolated patches of mostly undesirable land like tangled scrub forests thick with saw-palmetto, snake-filled pine flatwoods or impenetrable hammocks, the Cracker raised his meager crops and family in solitude. Houses were built from the land, cutting logs from nearby stands of pine or oak and dragging them to the home site with horses or oxen. The logs and lumber were shaped by hand and fitted one timber at a time. Rarely were there glass windows, and screens were just as scarce; this in a land where the mosquitos were so bad that "a man could swing a pint cup and catch a quart" of them.

A covered wagon caravan coming into North Florida in the early 1900s. Photograph, Florida State Archives.

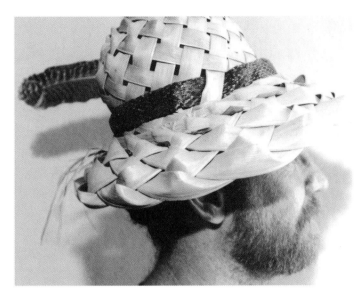

A contemporary Florida Cracker models a woven palmetto hat fashioned by Rasha Moore. Photograph by Roger Simms, 1997.

The stark material life of Crackers was a reflection of their make-do existence, which required that they fashion necessities from whatever was available. Soap was made from animal fat and lye, brooms from sage straw, and dishes from wood. The women made their own dresses out of cotton sacks, cut buttons out of gourds, and wove hats with palmettos.

Crackers were recycling long before it became popular to do so, making household items and garments out of the most unlikely of materials. Any salvaged metals were reshapened into tools, broken harnesses became belts, and cloth sacks were sewn into aprons and dresses. From Osceola County folklore is this story: "No grain is grown in these parts, and all feed ... is shipped in cotton bags. These bags are carefully saved by frugal families, bleached in the laundry and

> *"'Root hog or die poor' was a common expression used by those old crackers who I came up with, for there was a time when everyone had a job to do, no matter if it was the kids, for it took everyone in the family doing whatever had to be done in order to keep food on the table ... I've seen men with their clothes wet with sweat from clearing land with a grubbing hoe from sunup to sundown. I've watched them grow old before their time. I've seen these men and women together in a field with the sun beating down on them. Like I said, in those by-gone days, it was 'root hog or die poor.'"*
>
> — FLORIDA CRACKER AND AUTHOR CARL ALLEN EXPLAINING THE PHRASE "ROOT HOG OR DIE POOR," THE NAME OF HIS BOOK FROM WHICH THIS EXCERPT CAME.

Catfishing on the St. Johns

DeBary, Florida Cracker Jesse Otis Beall recalls the challenges and rewards of running a catfishing outfit on the St. Johns River in the 1950s: "Well, you done it for money and you done it for food - you done it for both. Cause a lot of times you'd catch bream and stuff there, naturally you'd take him home to eat it. You're not supposed to, but we always took the bream home and that's what we'd eat. The catfish we'd sell. We's gettin' about 30 cents a pound at the time for catfish then. But it's a hard living, it's a sorry fishing. You go out there and get crawfish out of a pond all day to bait two or three thousand hooks. It's work! It's work! And if you put grass shrimp on, it's work, I don't care. Boy, you tear your fingers up, big holes, everything. But we'd fish Lake Monroe, Lake Jessup, we'd fish everywhere. We followed fish. I started out here in the 50s and me and my friend we'd put out 10,000 hooks. We'd fish 5000 one day and I'd fish 5000 and he'd fish 5000. I said, well we can do that so we'll put 10,000 out. So we'd put 10,000 out. He'd fish 10,000 and I'd fish 10,000. We'd say well we're doin that

Catfish and mullet were Cracker staples throughout Florida.

let's put 30,000 out. Before it was over we had 40,000 fish hooks out there on Lake Monroe. I'd fish 10,000 one day and he'd fish 10,000. Next day we'd jump over on the other 10,000 and run them. And we was not baitin - they was bitin' empty hooks and we was dressing anywheres from twelve to thirteen hundred pounds a day of catfish.

We didn't dress them. We'd hire it done because there was too many of them we'd fish so long. We would carry them to the fish market and they would have people there to skin them. And then they would pay us off. But always in cash. We always liked that cash money. It was nice when you got a stack of bills like that, you always got as high as four, five hundred dollars at one time for a couple days work, you know.

Apron fashioned from a Rudy's Indiana Super-Corn cloth sack, c. 1920. Museum of Arts and Sciences collections. Gift of Gloria Burnell. Photograph by Roger Simms, 1997.

converted into all kinds of garments ... When I called on a [Cracker] woman, ... I found her wearing sackcloth made into a coarse work dress or smock, and not all the printing had been faded out, so that athwart her ample person she bore in faded pink letters the legend, 'The Perfect Form...' The 'ula' had been clipped from the last word."[4]

What few vegetables they harvested in their farmer-woodsman role were canned or dried for the winter, if they could. Game was preserved by smoking or by submerging meats, like a whole skinned raccoon, in a front-porch brine-filled barrel - a crude staved container which could very well have been the first "crackerbarrel." Lard spread around the lid sealed air out of the barrel.

Fifth generation Cracker Floridian Bill Dreggors recalls this method of storing meats as well as his regular attempts to avoid eating anything that came out of the saltwater: "And they had a big old

> *"Most Cracker fishermen observe a myriad of traditional taboos to ward off bad luck. For instance, it is bad luck to leave dock on a Friday, say 'alligator' or 'banana' on board, have a woman on board, whistle on board, turn the hatch upside down, or bring a black suitcase on board."*
>
> — FROM "THE CRACKERS" IN *SOUTH FLORIDA FOLKLIFE*. BY TINA BUCUVALAS, PEGGY A. BULGER, AND STETSON KENNEDY, 1994.

> *"He skinned his catch in the shade of a live-oak near the smoke-house. He tacked the hides, fur side down, against the walls. During the cool dry winter weather they cured quickly and rolled, salted bundles were ready every week to mail away or take to the itinerant buyer at Eureka."*
>
> — MARJORIE KINNAN RAWLINGS,
> *SOUTH MOON UNDER*, 1933.

barrel settin' up on the porch and in that barrel was all their meat. It was salted in brine and then just anything they'd kill, a coon, or a possum, or a squirrel, or anything they'd kill, they'd just clean it and throw it in that brine and weight it down with a brick on top of a board to keep it submerged. And we'd go there and my aunt (who kept the brine barrel) would say "You all want to stay for supper?" And she'd reach in there and pull out an old coon that was just wrinkled all up from that salt. And mom would say "I got to go home and cook for the rest of the family." I sure was proud, and I just couldn't think about having to eat anything that came out of that brine. But that's the only way they had to preserve food except to smoke it. Pork, now they could smoke pork in the smokehouse. But all the other food if they wanted to preserve it they had to put in that brine."[5] Venison and beef jerky

Cracker Flashlights

Author David M. Newell in his "If Nothin' Don't Happen" explains how Crackers got around in the woods at night without fancy lights and lanterns:

"When a feller wanted to travel through the Hammock at night, he could use dead cabbage-palm fans. The ground is covered with 'em and you can't hardly walk thirty steps without steppin' on one. They're real brittle and dry and burn like paper. You just pick one up by the stem, light the fan and it'll make a fine torch for a right good ways. Just before it burns out, you pick up another one, light it and go on. There ain't much danger of startin' a woods fire unless there's been a long dry spell. There ain't much undergrowth to catch fire in the Hammock and the ground is pretty soggy. And most always there's a good dew falls at night, so when we're through with a torch we just chunk it down."

Florida Cabbage Palm.

A Southern Cracker with his dogs. Because the coarse cloth used for work clothes and feed sacks soiled easily, Crackers dyed the material a dark blue using wild indigo. The settlers also used other natural dyes like tans from bay tree bark and browns from the blackjack oak. From Harper's New Monthly Magazine, *1857, p. 735.*

was made by soaking strips of meat in the brine for several days, then hanging them outside on a rack or the roof of the house to dry in the sun.

While they did little tromping across the moral high ground, Crackers were soundly based in their religious convictions. It has been said that early Cracker immigrants firmly kept the Sabbath and everything else they could lay their hands on.[6] But it is not clear which church they kept, if they kept one at all. Clark I. Cross suggests that what moral code the Crackers had was deeply rooted in their Protestant backgrounds.[7] It is more likely that, early on, Presbyterians were influential in the Cracker population with the less-structured Baptists dominating later, followed closely by the Methodists.[8] Along with their religious persuasions, Crackers continue to carry a long list of superstitions. For example, Crackers traditionally eat hog jowls and blackeye peas on New Year's Eve for good luck. It is believed that the more peas you eat the more success you will have in the upcoming year.

They grew everything they needed including rice. They raised rice in those old dry ponds over there. It was a good field place for rice for there'd be enough water in there to support it. And they grew their own tobacco, made their own chewin' tobacco and they had corn. They grew a lot of corn for cornmeal and for the animals too, for the stock. But of course the meat was wild meat and you didn't butcher cows partly because you couldn't afford to, and there was no where to keep it. The meat would spoil. Pork was the best. It could be preserved by smokin' it or saltin' it or brine it. And they grew their own vegetable gardens. They lived ... lived long enough to get me here anyhow. They rarely bought food just flour and coffee was about the biggest thing and brandy. And they all bought brandy. The records for the store down there in the 1870s my great uncle he would go there and he always bought brandy.

Fifth generation Cracker Floridian Bill Dreggors of DeLand.

— DELAND NATIVE BILL DREGGORS ON HIS
FLORIDA CRACKER ANTECEDENTS, NOVEMBER, 1996.

Cracker house of Jesse Dreggors (far right) at Crows Bluff, Lake County, Florida, c. 1905. The burlap-covered brine barrel in the foreground was used to preserve meats as there was no refrigerator in the Dreggors household. This photograph is from the collection of DeLand historian Bill Dreggors. Bill's great-grandfather John Dreggors with corncob pipe in hand is seated on the steps next to the brine barrel; his great uncle Jesse Dreggors is seated next to John. Four unidentified family members are seated in rocking chairs on the front porch behind a sleeping hound. The house, now gone, is well elevated by whole timber piers to allow cooling breezes to pass under the structure.

    Justice in the Cracker community was swift and often self-serving, with punition ranging from retaliation with fists and guns to recreational lynchings. Rarely was justice served by due process or by outside authorities. During the Florida Territorial period, Achille Murat observed this self-regulated style of Cracker law: "... There exists no form of government (and) every dispute is amicably terminated by the fist ... The land or their houses have, in their eyes, but a secondary value (to livestock) ... Each of these has its mark; and if any are stolen, he assembles his neighbors, and the proofs in hand, they go together to the thief, and administer to him a punishment more or less severe. According to their morality, cowstealing is the greatest crime."[9] This internal manner of administrating justice persisted well into the 1900s as Carl Dann points out: "(The Cracker) will seldom testify against the defendant (in a court of law), even though the crime was committed against him or his people. This is often true, even in case of a killing, but he will eventually square the account in his own way."[10] Castelnau in the late 1830s attempted to explain the reasons for this closed system, noting that Crackers of the period were not "checked by human laws - these cannot reach them in the midst of the woods, nor by

A wild hog hunting rattlesnakes. From Harper's New Monthly Magazine, *1855, p. 476. Feral hogs in Florida, called piney-woods rooters, are tenacious animals known for their poor temperament and for their unprovoked attacks on anything they happen to cross paths with, including people, bears, and rattlesnakes. Early on, Cracker settlers in the Florida scrub relied on the free-ranging hogs for food. Today, the hogs are still hunted with specialized dogs. Crackers like the famous hog-hunter Jimmy Summersill of Jacksonville spend weeks at a time catching and releasing hogs for sport, only occasionally taking one for food.*

religious principals that are totally unknown to them, these men know no other power than physical force, and no other pleasure than carrying out their brutal passions."[11] Marjorie Kinnan Rawlings in *South Moon Under* sums up nicely the purpose of Cracker self-policing: "... When a man was caught stealing, or lying to another's harm, he was dealt with ..., and the offender and the community were better and the more peaceful for the settling of the matter. They knew what they would tolerate and what they would not."[12] Lawlessness in contemporary rural Florida communities is mostly a thing of the past, although occasionally backcountry crimes like "cowstealing" are handled "out back."

Alligator Huntin'

Jesse Otis Beall, Cracker fisherman of DeBary, Florida has done just about everything to make a living including alligator poaching and commercial fishing. Alligator hunting was a way of life, albeit dangerous, for many Crackers like Jesse. There was a time when Jesse hunted alligators illegally as it was the only way to feed himself and his family back in the 1950s. It made them a little money which in turn put food on the table, so it was worth the risk, as Jesse tells it in this WCEU "Florida Crackerbarrel" (December 1996) interview.

Dana Ste.Claire: Jesse, you know you're about the most famous Cracker in these parts (DeBary) and, among other things, you are a well-known Cracker alligator hunter, and that's why we're here with you and the remnants of this gentleman (a very large alligator skull) ... he looks like he was about a 12-footer or so. There was a time when you did this for a living?

Jesse Otis Beall: That's the only thing we had to do. I mean I worked for the Oxfire Brush company when I was making 65 cents an hour, so we had to supplement some way, so I went to gator huntin'.

Ste.Claire: And exactly how do you hunt a gator?

Beall: Well, it all depends where I'm at. If I'm legal I can set hooks ... I'll set hooks for him. But where I couldn't do that, I'd pulled him out of a cave with a pole and killed him with a hatchet.

Ste.Claire: Now, you actually went back into the dens to get alligators?

Beall: Yes, just once. I went underwater. Went in the hole and hooked him and pulled him out. That gator was close to 12 foot long.

Ste.Claire: You actually swam underwater into the den and hooked the alligator?

DeBary, Florida Cracker and famous alligator hunter Jesse Otis Beall. Photograph by Diane Gilpatrick, 1997.

Jesse Dreggors alligator hunting on the St. Johns River, c. 1905. Photograph from the collection of Bill Dreggors.

Beall: And hooked him. I had a rope tied to the pole and came back out and pulled him out.

Ste.Claire: I'd say that you were either brave, very brave, or very hungry.

Beall: Both! Cause I wasn't scared of him and I think the alligators knew that. I just was not ascared of him. I could wade in a hole with one and not be feared, no fear a'tall and I think he was ascared of me more than I was of him.

Ste.Claire: And every once in a while the game warden would come around ...?

Beall: Oh yes! Oh yes! I'll tell you you one story. Now me and a friend of mine, Pete, we was huntin' on a creek, years ago, and I seen a game warden come across the lake. I knowed who he was, it was Charlie Clark. And Pete says, "Man let's get out of here." And I said "No," I said, "I'm not goin to run because I know Charlie ... and he might hurt himself." He was an old man then and he come on shore and I had a big old (gator-hooking) rod that I stuck down in the ground before he got here. He came up and pulled that rod up, stuck it back down in the ground and put his foot on it, and I had a backpack on my back and I had gator hooks in it and mullet head what I baited the hooks with and he asked me, he said "Can I look in there?" I said "Well, sure." And I know he was going to look anyhow, so he looks in there and closed it back up. And he said "You know, Jesse, I could arrest you for takin' a gator." I said "Why?" He said "Cause you got the tools to do it."

Ste.Claire: But you had run from him a couple of times, too.

Beall: Oh yes, I did a lot of times!

Ste.Claire: You told me once how you knew those river channels and you knew exactly where to go to get away.

Beall: I knew where to go and I could tear their boats up in a heartbeat, cause I know where to go around things, and their boats would hit it.

Ste.Claire: And that's exactly what would happen too, and that's how you would lose them. You would go through one of those river channels and miss the boat that was sunk below the water and they would hit it. I've talked to the old game wardens!

Beall: And then I'd go home (laughing).

Ste.Claire: Well, now we should also point out for the record that you were hunting alligator for hides only. You weren't hunting them for the meat. That only happened later on. Florida Crackers really never ate alligator meat, did they? That became popular when, about the 1950s?

Beall: It was the 50s and early 60s. Yep. We ate some. Don't get me wrong now 'cause when we hunted, when we be out in the swamp five or six miles out

A Florida swamp "infested" with alligators.

in there you could not tote that meat back out there 'cause it was too much. Time you toted that hide out of there you was so thirsty you would even drink out of a cow track. And to get it out you just had to do what you had to do.

Ste.Claire: *So you were taking the hides right there where you hunted the alligators. Were they bringing a pretty good price back then?*

Beall: *Three dollars fifteen cents a foot.*

Ste.Claire: *And you'd get a little bit more if you stretched them, right Jesse?*

Beall: *And I'd a stretched them too, buddy! They got on to me one time about it when I stretched them too much, you know, and they said "You can't do that" and I said "You want my hides, you'll take them." Most of them they took them ... about four or five hide buyers. They said just don't stretch 'em or we just won't pay you for 'em. So I quit it.*

Ste.Claire: *Well, thank you for telling me about cracker Florida alligator poaching and hunting. I know you did some of it legally too!*

Beall: *I done that for the meat!*

The hard life of a Cracker was soon forgotten when it came time for occasional pleasures. These were usually social gatherings like an evening dance or more often a day-long outdoor feast. Most of the get-togethers were family-style and took place in the light of the day, like the *perleu*, an extended cookout of sorts. At a *perleu*, the Cracker women would bring large pots, lots of chickens, rice and biscuits. The chickens were boiled over open fires until they were nearly done and then rice was added. The feast was served with coffee made over the same fire. Around the cooking activities, Crackerfolks would carry on in "all-day sings" and contests. A similar event was the Florida Frolic, an all-day wild game feast. At a Frolic, the men and boys would arrive early, grouping at a predetermined location, and begin to hunt and fish. Their "catches" were carried to the Frolic and cooked by the women who had already begun preparing grits, palmetto cabbage, succotash and coffee.

"You may have been born and bred in Georgia, but you're nothin' but a crumb here."

— AN ANONYMOUS FLORIDA CRACKER.
FROM THE STETSON KENNEDY FILES,
FLORIDA STATE ARCHIVES.

A *cane grind* was popular in areas that grew sugar cane, like the south Florida region. The *grind* usually took place in the fall and coincided with the harvesting of the sugar cane. Crackers would come together for the day to sit around and chew cane, drink hot cane juice, tell stories and sing. Cane syrup was cooked along with everything else and would be taken at the end of a meal by "sopping" it up with a biscuit. A very potent cane beer, made from the fermented skimmings from boiling syrup, and a sticky "polecat" froth were available for the taking, too.

The beginnings of a chicken perleu.

The Cracker custom of gathering socially was a way for neighbors who were isolated from each other by great distances to connect from time to time. It provided social harmony to some degree, but more important, it created the means for secluded Cracker settlers to bond with each other, reinforcing their traditions, beliefs and way of life.

A cane grind in Pasco County, probably Dade City, c. 1915. Photograph, Florida State Archives.

Cracker Wash Day

Wash day before the invention of modern-day appliances was literally this - an all-day affair, and one that folks weren't particularly fond of. The long and tiring work required to clean clothes long ago becomes plainly evident judging by the early appliances and wash-related gizmos and gadgets Crackers had to use. Back then, cleaning your clothes wasn't a simple matter of loading a washing machine, turning it on, and walking away. Soiled clothes early on were "cooked" clean in large iron kettles or copper boilers, a process which required constant attention throughout the day. Boiling was one of few effective ways to remove ground-in dirt and stains from clothes that were worn for sometimes weeks and months

Cracker wash day required long hours of boiling and scrubbing.

Clothes sticks like this 1879 Eastlake model were used to lift garments from boiling water, among other things. From Scientific American, *December, 1879.*

at a time. This was by far the most common method of washing clothes by Crackers, as most could not afford the next level of technology, even if it was available.

Long washsticks were used to stir and swish the clothes around in lye water (with a little soap mixed in), and then used to lift the clothes out of the boiling solution. Even when factory-produced manual and mechanical washers came on to the American farm scene, boiling usually preceded washing. Heavy-duty scrubbers and washboards were used with strong detergents to "finish out" the clothes in a washtub. Next, the garments were rinsed in clean water and passed through a ringer, if one was available, to squeeze out excess water. Finally, the clothes were collected in a basket and dried on the line or over the fence.

One of the earliest and simplest "household" wash appliances was the double-tub wash stand made in the late 19th century. Dual galvanized tubs were used to scrub clothes after they were boiled and stirred in a big kettle. The

The 1904 manually-operated Automatic Washing Machine manufactured by the Boss Washing Machine Co. From Her *magazine, January, 1909.*

Cracker wash day in the tool shed, c. 1900. A wash bench with galvanized tubs and a clothes wringer is seen to the right. The lower photograph shows an unidentified man rinsing clothes in a galvanized tub mounted on a wooden barrel. Photographs, Florida State Archives.

wooden stand for the tubs was ingeniously made to collapse, folding up for easy storage.

Wash day was made a little easier during the industrial revolution when American inventors produced an endless array of mechanized washers, from 19th century hand-powered appliances to early 20th century gasoline and electric engine-driven machines. One of these "state-of-the-art" appliances was the Maytag gasoline power washer made in 1926 by the Maytag Company, Newton, Iowa. This cast-aluminum, gasoline engine-run Maytag washer, engaged by a

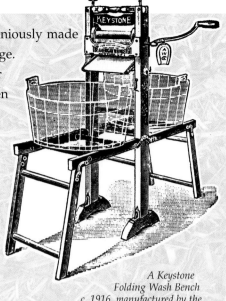

A Keystone Folding Wash Bench c. 1916, manufactured by the American Wringer Co. From the Excelsior Stove & Mfs. Co. Catalog, 1916.

motorcycle-like kick-starter, was widely marketed for its versatility. The washer came with special attachments, including a meat-grinder and an ice cream churn, which were powered by the same gear that ran the washing agitator. The "famous" Maytag was also advertised for its labor-saving operation with a marketing campaign aimed at the farm wife - "the time saved can be spent with your children, with your garden or your chicks."

An endless array of gadgets

Maytag Gas-Operated Wooden Washer c. 1914. From an original Maytag advertisement, collection of Dave and Gloria Burnell.

were produced as accessories, many of which posted some thinly veiled commercialism. For example, a Silk Hosiery Wash-Board made in 1920 by the Real Silk Hosiery Mills Company in Indianapolis as a Procter & Gamble premium, came with clear instructions on the back of the washboard that required the washer to "use Ivory Soap Flakes exclusively." Another clever device, and one that quickly became a necessity, was a circa 1915 ringer prod made by Blackstone Mfg. Co. of Jamestown, N.Y. Ringer feeders like this one were manufactured by the thousands when housewives began to injure their fingers in mechanical clothes ringers. One of the more unusual washday gadgets produced was a turn-of-the-century necktie-ringer used to squeeze the excess water out of neckties, back when you could wash them, if you had them.

Cracker dances were not as common, but when they happened they were well attended by settlers from miles around. Sometimes they lasted for several days at a time. All night dancing was an adults-only event and typically the children were grouped together in the late evening inside an outbuilding or at the back of the dance barn to sleep, if they could. Self-described Florida Cracker Carl Dann in his *Vicissitudes and Casathrophics* (1929) gives us the lowdown on the breakdown and the nuances of Cracker dance etiquette: "I have attended many 'Cracker breakdowns' that lasted three days and nights. You would dance until you tired, then sleep a while, then up and dance some more. The music for a real country square dance is one fiddle and a second man who would beat the fiddle straws. A real 'Cracker' square dancer had a little jig all his own that he does on the corner

> *"You can take a 'Cracker' out of the woods, but you can't take the woods out of a 'Cracker.'"*
>
> — CARL DANN
> *VICISSITUDES AND CASATHROPHICS*, 1929.

before he swings his partner, or at any time when he has the chance ... At a real 'Cracker Shindig' a man keeps dancing. You would see jigging, clog dancing and the Highland Fling and other steps that you never saw before. You would see no loving on the side; no trips made out to the buggy for the flask. You would not see a girl take a drink or smoke; you would, perhaps, see a number of old ladies smoking pipes, but never the daughter." Dann also points out that Cracker dances, when they happened, were a must-do event: "When I would hear of a 'Cracker Six' dance, if I could not borrow a horse and buggy, I would

A Cracker social gathering at a one room log school house in northern Volusia County, Florida, c. 1900. Photograph, Florida State Archives, gift of Bill Dreggors, DeLand, Florida.

take my last dollar, if necessary, to rent one, and drive all day long through the sand in order to reach a dance by dark. I would dance all night and drive back the next day; twelve hours dancing and twenty-four riding."[13]

Going to town was entertainment for Crackers, too. Bartering for and buying what "store boughten" goods they could afford usually comprised the business of the day and was the purpose for the long trek into town, but Crackers enjoyed the attractions of civilization, at least occasionally when such trips were required, and prepared themselves for the event with great anticipation. Tampa historian Tony Pizzo relays this account of the special day in the 19th century: "Saturday was 'going-to-town' day for the people of the outlying areas. The visiting 'crackers' congregated in the business district ... They came in their 'two-wheeled carts' drawn by a horse, a mule, or an ox, with the driver astride the animal, the load of cotton, hide, or other produce was piled on the cart; if there were woman or children, they were perched on top of the load."[14] John Tidball, a United States officer stationed in Florida in 1849, observed and recorded a Ocala-bound Cracker procession in remarkable detail, noting a certain protocol among the sojourners:

"Each of these 'cracker' families boasted the possession of a mule or an old

Crackers and their wagons caused traffic jams during their Saturday town gatherings. From The Great South *by Edward King, 1875, p. 314.*

horse ... Little more than skin and bones. They also had some rickety contrivance, called by way of flattery a cart, made up of a pair of old wheels, and a combination of poles, clapboard and ropes. Every Saturday all of the families from far and near came into the town ostensibly to do what little shopping their circumstances demanded ... It was sort of a gala occasion, but why Saturday should have been selected in preference to any other day was a mystery to me ... But Saturday have by common consent become the day, and so continued, and motley crowd it brought to town. Each family formed a little procession of its own, all in single file, with the head of the household leading off, with his long rifle on his shoulder. He was a curious specimen of humanity, almost always tall and gaunt with legs much too long in proportion to his body, hunched up shoulders and caved in chest, and a little round belly like a pot sticking out in front. A ragged shirt and trousers, a pair of brogans without stockings, and an old wool hat from beneath which protruded lanky locks of sunburnt hair, made up the outward man. This specimen of genus homo was followed by the elder sons, each with his gun and in general a counterpart of their sire. Then came the cart - the family carriage - driven by a half clad urchin mounted on the back of the horse or mule with his knees drawn up and his feet resting on the shafts. In the cart rode those of the family too young or too feeble to walk; and these shared the limited space of the clap-board buggy with the whiskey jug and two or three dry hides brought along for barter. Sometimes they had a few coon or other skins also. Following the cart came the female portion of the family, the mother always at the head, followed by the daughters

Ted Smallwood in front of his southwest Florida store which also served as the Chokoloskee post office, c. 1930. Photograph courtesy of Smallwood's Store Museum collection.

in the order of age. The garb of these females, always the scantiest patterns was picturesque with ingenious patching of many colors; but true to feminine instinct they generally showed some attempt at tidying up for the occasion. Two, three, or more mangy and hungry looking dogs brought up the rear of this unique procession and there they trudged silently along the hot and sandy road, scarcely a word spoke ..."[15]

In town, the dry goods store served as important nexus for Cracker peoples to discuss and argue life, the weather, the crops, town business, and politics. In the late 19th century and early 20th century, there were few institutions which influenced the American scene more than the crossroads general store. Here, people from every socioeconomic strata, including the heads of Cracker families, would sit, swap yarns, and arrive at an unofficial consensus on the issues of the day. It was not uncommon at these gatherings for the shopkeep or talkative patrons to dispense heavy doses of homespun wisdom or philosophize on the issues at hand, all while sitting atop large wooden soda cracker barrels. This is where the term "cracker-barrel philosopher" comes from, but the cracker part describes the barrels and not the sitters.

Rarely was food purchased from the town store by Crackers. Instead, what little money they had was used to buy necessities, things which could not be procured from their immediate surroundings, like shells for their shotguns and real coffee. But some money was almost always set aside for pure "store-boughten" pleasures, mainly whiskey and tobacco: "First of all the jug was filled with the weekly supply of whiskey of a grade costing in those days (1849 - 1850) only about twenty cents per gallon. Even at this rate the poverty of these people caused them to be temperate, though never totally abstentious. Tobacco and snuff were the next items of consideration; for the men all chewed, the women all dipped, and both men and women smoked pipes."[16] Margaret Deland in her *Florida Days* (1889) sizes up well the allure of tobacco: "The household of a Cracker family dispenses often with necessities, - perhaps because they are considered luxuries; while the comforts which it enjoys might be summed up in one word, tobacco."[17]

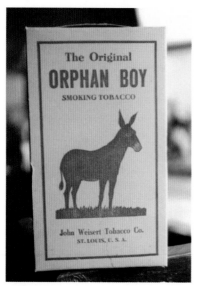

Orphan Boy smoking tobacco box, c. 1900. Photograph by Roger Simms, 1997.

The country store was an important gathering place for Crackers who often lived at great distances from each other. It was here that settlers caught up on the latest regional news and gossip. From Harper's New Monthly Magazine, *1884, p. 405.*

The store variety of whiskey provided endless pleasure to Crackers, as well, and in some cases to great excess. John Claiborne in his 1841 profile of the backwoods-man, *A Trip through the Piney Woods,* offers up a profile of Crackers having no restraint and little ambition, suggesting that the Crackers in his neck of woods enjoyed partaking in drink, but were too lazy to make their own moonshine. Instead, he claims, "they prefer to tramp to the nearest groggery with a gallon-jug on their shoulders, which they get filled with 'bust-head,' 'rot-gut,' or some other equally poisonous abomination; and then tramp home again, reeling as they trudge along, laughing idiotically, or shouting like mad in a glorious state of beastly intoxication."[18] Carl Dann, on the other hand, would have us believe that Cracker drunkenness and belligerence was not as epidemic as outsiders made it out to be: "Once in a while you might see some 'Cracker' drunk, but he would come to the dance drunk and he would not last long, as he was not welcome. You would see a little shooting, perhaps, once in a while, or a rare cutting scrape, but not often."[19]

Cracker Tobacco

Tobacco smoking was a pure Cracker pleasure and favorite pastime of both men and some women. Enoch Vann, a Madison County, Florida lawyer and candidate for office in 1860, recalls his encounter with pipe-smoking Cracker at a country dance while trying to collect votes: "A (Cracker) girl ..., breathing heavily and in full perspiration, asked me if I was almost through smoking. I apologized, and was about to pocket my pipe when she informed me that she would like to smoke a little herself. I again apologized for not offering my pipe before - carefully wiped the stem on my coat tail and handed the pipe to her with a polite bow. She puffed away until she had to move up. She wiped the stem under her arm and returned the pipe to me and galloped off. Of course, I commenced smoking right off - for I do not know how many voters were looking on, whose votes I would have lost."
— ENOCH VANN *REMINISCENCES OF A GEORGIA-FLORIDA-PINEWOODS CRACKER LAWYER.*

From *Seventy Years in Dixie* by F. D. Srygley, 1891.

Few Crackers could afford "store-boughten" goods, and when they could it was usually tobacco, salt, coffee, flour, ammunition and sometimes whiskey. This photograph of rural Cracker storetender Mr. Keyes illustrates supplies typically available at a mid-20th century Florida country store, including boxes of crackers, which has nothing whatsoever to do with the naming of Crackers. Photograph, Dan Biferie.

Cracker Staples

Long ago, Cracker farm folks had to rely on homemade goods for everyday living. Because grocery stores were often difficult to reach and even harder to afford, rural people found it easier to make certain foods and household items, such as butter and candles. Both of these products were important staples for 19th century families.

Rural Cracker settlers were self-reliant peoples who grew their own food and made their own household items. Florida State Archives photograph, c. 1960. Gift of Nixon Smiley.

Butter was made from milk taken from the one or two cows a farmer would tend for dairy products, if they had them. A variety of churns, including a wooden barrel-type and upright stoneware and wood staved containers, turned, shook, rocked or dashed cream into butter. The remaining fat-free liquid became buttermilk and was stored separately. The butter was washed in cold water, worked to remove excess liquid, and finally mixed with salt.

Wooden paddles and special knives were used to work the butter into its final consistency and to pack it into crocks and tubs for storage. The finest butter was made through great care. A mass of butter was worked back and forth in a large spouted bowl, being pushed and pulled until the desired thickness was achieved and excess liquid was drained.

On some farms, intricately decorated wooden molds were used to shape butter for market and tabletop presentation. Most common were the plunger-type molds. A wooden tamp, a type of flat-headed masher, was used to pack butter into the mold bowl. A carved plate impressed a design into the butter. After the butter was set in the mold, it was pushed out by the plunger in decorated form.

Mold designs made the butter more attractive for sale at the local market. The decorations, such as birds, flowers, and cows, identified the farm where the butter was made. Buyers who preferred butter from a certain farm looked for a special mark.

The earliest method of candle-making required repeated dippings into melted tallow (animal fat) or wax. A later method used a mold, usually made of soldered tin in a variety of sizes, to form the candles.

After the wick was inserted, melted wax or tallow was poured through the openings of the mold and allowed to harden. Later, the filled mold was placed briefly into hot water to loosen the candles. Then, the finished candles were lifted from the mold by their wicks.

Candles were an important household item because they were the only source of light in most rural homes. Through the 19th century and early 20th century, candles were gradually replaced by kerosene and whale oil-burning lamps.

All told, Crackers were strongly individualistic and self-reliant, yet generous and proud even in poverty. These age-old character traits shaped a poor but courageous population of backwoods settlers who, long ago, carved out a life from a hostile land and, in turn, provided a spirited foundation for the peopling of the rural South.

Cracker Dyes

Because the coarse cloth used for work clothes and feed sacks soiled easily, Crackers commonly dyed materials dark blue using wild indigo. The settlers also made other natural dyes like tans from bay tree bark and browns from the blackjack oak, and beautiful reds from a ladybug-sized insect called the cochineal. The bug, brought to America by the Minorcan settlers of the 1768 British colony of New Smyrna, Florida, produced one of the most attractive colors for garments, but processing it into dye was laborious. It took some 70,000 of the female insects to make a single pound of dye. Native plant specialist Georgia Zern compiled this list of natural dyes used long ago by Florida settlers, as well as some of the techniques involved in dying with natural materials. Mordants, she explains, help the dyes combine with the fabric to make a more or less permanent color bond. Some common mordants are alum, chrome and tin; back then, urine was often used.

Acorns - Soak acorns in water several days. Boil for one hour, strain from dyebath. Put in mordanted wool or cloth. Boil for 30-45 minutes. Alum gives a poor tan, chrome an olive, iron grays it and tin gives a yellow.

Aster - The small white aster that blooms in October and November gives a beautiful rich yellow dye with an alum mordant; with chrome, a soft gold.

Bayberry - Bruise and boil berries for a long time. Boiled water will yield a blue dye for unmordanted cloth or wool. When coppers are added, dark brown is attained and walnut leaves, hulls or bark will produce black. The leaves with an alum mordant gives a yellow brown or light yellow depending on the amount of leaves used, one pound leaves for light yellow, one and a half for brown. Leaves should be dried.

Broomsedge - Chop and boil the dried grass for twenty minutes, put in wet mordanted cloth or wool. Alum gives a clear light greenish yellow, chrome produces a brassy color. Good for indigo, overdye for green.

Camphor Tree - The leaves give a good shade of tan - with alum, a light tan, with chrome, a darker tan and tin, a yellow tan.

Cedar - The root of the common red cedar yields a purple dye.

Cherry - The roots of wild cherry give a reddish purple to alum mordanted cloth. Two pounds of roots to one pound of wool. The bark gives shades of yellow to orange to tan.

Chrysanthemum - The yellow variety yields a good brass color with alum mordanted cloth. Break off plant at root and use entire plant, leaves and blossoms.

Dog Fennel - The fernlike leaves yield a bright greenish yellow with alum, tin, a pale yellow and chrome, a duller yellow.

Elderberry - The color from the berries varies in intensity depending on the amount used and length of boiling - longer boiling deepens the color. To obtain an even color, enter wet wool quickly while continually stirring. To a peck of berries, bruised and boiled thirty minutes, add one tablespoon salt. Strain out fruit before dyeing. Alum gives a lilac blue, chrome a violet purple. The leaves shredded and bruised give shades of yellow with both alum and chrome.

Fleabane - Chrome gives a gold color, alum a buttercup yellow, tin a brighter yellow. Green can be had by adding 1/2 teaspoon copperas to dye bath. Predye and remove to add chemical then reenter cloth for 30 minutes. The whole plat is used, break off at roots and into short lengths and simmer 45 minutes, strain and then enter cloth for 45 minutes.

Grape Leaves - Boil leaves a long time. Alum gives a yellow green, tin a gold and chrome a gray-tan green.

Hickory - The inner bark yields a greenish yellow with alum, dark yellow with chrome and tin a bright yellow. To make the dye, a half bushel of bark is boiled for two hours and then strained. Cream of tartar added to dye bath brightens all colors.

Indigo - The Spanish, Minorcans, English and French transported favorite plants and animals to the New World. Some of the most important plants brought to Florida were citrus, especially oranges, figs, rice, sugarcane and indigo. These were grown as cash crops for the early settlers. Indigo in particular was very profitable. Originating in India and Egypt, early settlers found suitable growing conditions here in Florida. The plant, while growing profusely, required lengthy processing to make indigo dye. At one time, an ounce of indigo was worth more than an equal amount of gold. But only the wealthy could afford this beautiful blue cloth, hence the terms "royal blue" and "bluebloods."

Mimosa - A large pail of leaves boiled for one hour yields dye for two pounds of yarn, strain off leaves first. Alum gives a bright yellow, chrome deep gold and tin a brassy yellow. With the addition of one teaspoon copperas to dye bath a beautiful dark green can be obtained with all mordants. If water is not hard add a teaspoon of lime to the dyebath.

Pokeberry - Gives a nice shade of red if mordanted with vinegar. If not enough berries are used then a salmon orange results. The dye bath must be stirred continually to get even coverage.

Sumac - For a gray, soak half a peck of berries one hour, boil 45 minutes, strain and add cold water to make 4 gallons. Warm again, immerse cloth and keep at boil for 30 minutes. Remove cloth, add 1 teaspoon copperas and soak 15 minutes. Vinegar and rusted iron can replace the copperas. Chrome gives a green gold and alum yellow.

Suggested Reading

Marjorie Kinnan Rawlings, *Cross Creek*. New York: Charles Scribner's Sons, 1942.

Patrick D. Smith, *A Land Remembered*. Sarasota: Pineapple Press, 1984.

Notes

1. Letter of June 27, 1766, from Colonial official Gavin Cochrane to the Earl of Dartmouth.

2. Comte de Castelnau, "Essay on Middle Florida, 1837 - 1838," *Florida Historical Quarterly* 26 (January 1948), p. 236.

3. Frank Hatheway Diary, January 18, 1846, cited in James M. Denham, "The Florida Cracker Before the Civil War as Seen Through Travelers' Accounts." *Florida Historical Quarterly* 72, no. 4 (April 1994), p. 459.

4. Stetson Kennedy files, Florida State Archives, Tallahassee.

5. Bill Dreggors, interview November 1996, Port Orange, Florida.

6. Anonymous observation about Crackers in Delma E. Presley, "The Crackers of Georgia," 1976, p. 105.

7. Clark I. Cross, "The Florida Cracker," in *Born of the Sun*, eds. Joan E. Gill and Beth R. Read, 1975, p. 137.

8. Delma E. Presley, "The Crackers of Georgia," 1976, p. 105.

9. Achille Murat, *United States of North America*, 1833, p. 54

10. Carl Dann, *Vicissitudes and Casathrophics*, 1929, p. 74

11. Comte de Castelnau, "Essay on Middle Florida, 1837 - 1838," *Florida Historical Quarterly* 26 (January 1948), p. 236.

12. Marjorie Kinnan Rawlings, *South Moon Under*. New York: Ballantine Books, 1933, p. 193.

13. Carl Dann, *Vicissitudes and Casathrophics*, 1929, pp. 71 - 72.

14. Anthony P. Pizzo, *Tampa Town 1824 - 1886: The Cracker Village with a Latin Accent*, 1968.

15. John Tidball, "Florida, 1849 - 50," John Tidball Papers, United States Military Academy, West Point, New York, cited in James M. Denham, "Cracker Woman and Their Families in Nineteenth Century Florida," in *Florida's Heritage of Diversity: Essays in Honor of Samuel Proctor*. Mark I. Greenberg, William Warren Rogers, and Canter Brown, Jr., editors. Tallahassee: Sentry Press, 1997.

16. John Tidball, ibid.

17. Margaret Deland, *Florida Days*. Boston: Little, Brown, and Co., 1889, p. 178.

18. John F. H. Clairborne, "A Trip through the Piney Woods (1841)," *Mississippi Historical Society Publications 9*, 1906, p. 514.

19. Carl Dann, *Vicissitudes and Casathrophics*, 1929, p. 73.

The Clark Homestead, c. 1880s, Maytown, Florida. Photograph, Dana Ste.Claire, 1996.

Shotguns and Saddlebags: Cracker Architecture in Old Florida

"Crackers make the most unsuitable houses you can imagine. I knew a tree to fall on one and beat it right down to the ground, cupboard, crockery and all. A family would be more safe in the crust of a pumpkin, and about as well sheltered from the weather as a hen coop"

— ELLEN BROWN, A NEW HAMPSHIRITE WHO
IMMIGRATED TO EAST FLORIDA, 1839.

It could be said that a good definition of a Cracker house is any house that a Cracker lived in, as these rural settlers throughout Florida history have sheltered themselves in a mix of structures, some less formally designed than others. They had colorful names like Single-Pen, Saddlebag, Dog-Trot, and Shotgun - a shack in which all of its rooms are in direct line with each other, so that a shot fired from the front porch could exit the through the back door without hitting anything in the house.

Crackers mostly relied on building materials available from their immediate surroundings, and dwellings of rough log construction or with palmetto-thatched roofs and sides, for example, were not uncommon. Achille Murat in the early 19th century notes these Cracker houses were typically "huts (which) may easily be constructed in two or three days."[1] In *Cross Creek*, Marjorie Kinnan Rawlings elaborates on this manner of construction, a type not unlike that which was used by earlier Florida Native Americans:

"The (house) was a palmetto shack, no larger than six feet by eight. The four corners were sapling cypresses. Palmetto fronds joined these to make walls and were thatched overhead for a roof.

"This is what they call a two-barreled shotgun shack."

— ANONYMOUS FLORIDA CRACKER,
STETSON KENNEDY FILES,
FLORIDA STATE ARCHIVES.

Cockroaches ran among the fronds and darted inside the dark box of a home. There was a half-door, the lower half made from a crate and the upper of burlap sacking. I lifted the sacking and saw he had built a sapling bunk along one side. The pallet on it was filled with moss. A ragged quilt was the only cover. A small rusty stove stood opposite the bunk, its pipe lifting crookedly and precariously above the dry palmetto thatching."[2] With the palmetto thatching of these types of "huts" came a host of unwanteds as Charles Pierce explains: "Palmetto fans made a good roof but had to be replaced every two or three years. It was a dry and cool house, but there were others who liked the palmetto leaves also. Roaches, lizards, and small snakes all made their homes in them, fortunately not many snakes but plenty of roaches and lizards of all sizes and kinds."[3]

Crackers who camped on the outskirts of civilization sometimes hastily constructed shanties from whatever they could salvage from piles of discarded building materials, collapsed houses, and town dumps.

Unlike styled architecture, Cracker structures were rarely elaborate and evolved slowly over time, with changes usually prompted by necessity, like a growing family, for example. Interestingly, the worn look of any of these home-made Cracker houses seems to be an inherent characteristic of the people who built them.

Today, architects have a more formal description for Cracker houses and what makes them typically Cracker. This definition emerged mainly through Ron Haase's work, *Classic Cracker: Florida's Wood-Frame Vernacular Architecture* (1992) which provided architects and historians with a

Crackers fashioned many of their houses and furniture from natural materials found in their immediate surroundings.

The John Wiley Hill home, a traditional "double pen" log home in Homeland, Florida, c. late 19th century. Photograph, Florida State Archives.

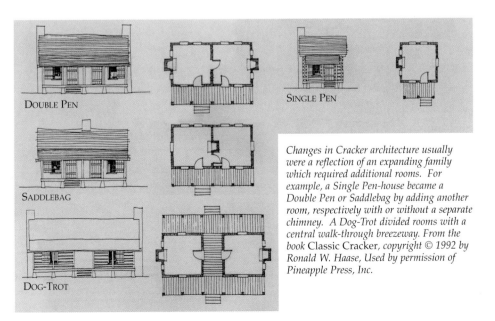

DOUBLE PEN

SINGLE PEN

SADDLEBAG

Changes in Cracker architecture usually were a reflection of an expanding family which required additional rooms. For example, a Single Pen-house became a Double Pen or Saddlebag by adding another room, respectively with or without a separate chimney. A Dog-Trot divided rooms with a central walk-through breezeway. From the book Classic Cracker, *copyright © 1992 by Ronald W. Haase, Used by permission of Pineapple Press, Inc.*

DOG-TROT

good typology of the vernacular Cracker architecture found throughout the state. What is considered to be the characteristic Florida Cracker building dates back to the early 19th century (later dates have been suggested; see Note no. 4) when settlers began to build crude houses of familiar Euro-American design, but with Deep South modifications, like one-story bungalows or two-story hall and parlor homes with large, wraparound porches.

The Cracker house design evolved in the Southeastern United States in response to the hot and humid, often unbearable, summer weather. Vernacular architecture helped keep occupants comfortable during the sultriest of dog days. Steeply pitched roofs ensured good ventilation above high ceilings and deep porches and wide overhangs provided plenty of shade throughout the day. Tall and often paired windows, usually screenless, were used to cross-

"But it wasn't until I trekked from Pensacola to Key West and from Micanopy to Marianna visiting house after house that a pattern of significance began to appear. Before that time I had seen too many picturesque Victorians and asymmetrical saltboxes to catch on to the purity of form in the basic Cracker farmhouse. I had not isolated in my mind's eye the initial symmetry and classic simplicity that each Cracker farmhouse began with. My vision was obscured by the vagueries of a porch half filled-in to add a bedroom or a shed added to provide needed storage or the sophistication of an indoor toilet. With time, the closing-in of an open dog-trot, and other such compositional adjustments, nullified in my mind the initial classic clarity of these forms. Now I looked closer, peeling back to find the bare essentials, the basic beginnings, the essential form that one son had constructed in reaction to the tradition of this father's house."

— RONALD W. HAASE, "A PERSONAL SEARCH FOR CRACKER FLORIDA," IN *FLORIDA ARCHITECT*, JANUARY/FEBRUARY 1987, PP. 26 - 27.

"There is an Old Florida, call it Cracker Florida if you will, where a distinctive way of life and attitudes persist, where houses and barns seem little changed but this Florida exists only in pockets and seems harder to find with every passing year."

— CLARK I. CROSS, *THE FLORIDA CRACKER*, 1975.

ventilate the interiors of a house. Even the loosely-fitted cypress shingles allowed air to circulate through the roof and simple board-and-batten or clapboard siding provided additional ventilation around the house.

Breezeways and dog-trots, a type of open corridor connecting front and back doors, were commonly used to channel any wind through the "middle" of the house. These

> *"(Cracker houses are) mostly log-huts ... sometimes they fill in the cavities by nailing strips of thin boards between every two courses of the logs, most of them, however do not take the trouble."*
>
> — U. S. Army Lieutenant John Greble on Cracker houses between Palatka and Tampa, 1854.

central, open hallways were also important in separating the main house from the kitchen, because hearths and wood-burning stoves generated much heat and occasionally fires.

A dog trot separates the house and kitchen of the Williams place near Cedar Creek, Baker County, Florida. An early pitcher pump is mounted to the rail of the dog trot. Photograph, Florida State Archives. Gift of the Baker County Historical Society.

Weathering Old Florida:
A Historical Account of Summer Sufferance

While Florida has changed dramatically over the last century, it has remained in many ways the same. It is a known and accepted fact, for example, that Floridians, particularly those who have settled the tropical regions of the state, will forever be plagued in the summer by inclement

In 1892, shade trees were left standing over this Cracker house on the Ocklawaha River a few miles down run of Silver Springs. Photograph, Florida State Archives. Gift of the Lake County Historical Association.

weather and swarms of pesky insects. Alas, living in the Sunshine State means more than mild winters.

These days, modern household conveniences shut out much of the summer heat and humidity, and most of the bugs. Imagine, though, having to live through a hot and buggy Florida August without the comforts of air-conditioning or sans window screens. But it wasn't too long ago when luxuries like climate-control devices, fans and refrigerators were nothing more than fleeting thoughts in the minds of distressed Southerners.

Florida folks have a long and colorful history of modifying their living environments to make themselves more comfortable in the summertime. Stories abound of historical characters who were driven by the heat and insects into local rivers, some turned stark raving mad by the elements.

Architectural designs were employed early on to cope with the warm weather. For example, tried and true Cracker features were incorporated into the construction designs of many 19th century houses. Breezeways, or open corridors which channeled wind through the "middle" of a house, wide verandas, steeply pitched roofs, and large windows were just a few of the Cracker elements added to houses to ensure maximum cooling during even the hottest of summer days.

Staying cool was one thing, albeit difficult; bugs were a different matter altogether. There was a time when fine window screen was unknown or too dear to buy, and early homesteaders were faced with the unsettling choice of keeping out the insects or opening the windows and letting in whatever breeze there was. And as any resident will tell you, Florida hosts swarms of seasonal pests which are drawn to open windows. Frequent summertime flyers include very large mosquitos and smaller ones which are equally as awful, house flies, deer flies, yellow flies, black flies, horse flies, and surely the worst of the lot, "noseeums," the seemingly ever-present sand gnats.

Later, the ability for Southerners to cope with their surroundings was made easier during the industrial revolution when a host of clever 19th century American inventors produced an endless array of devices to help people better handle the inconveniences of Southern life ... and, of course, to make a little money in the process. Floridians who were consumed with beating the summer heat and bugs spent hard-earned money on these contraptions, some of which worked for more than a day.

An early 19th century glass fly trap.

Most of these devices were designed to keep bugs out of the kitchen. House flies were always regular visitors, so many gadgets were offered specifically to prevent them from getting to and spoiling food. As an example, a fashionable blown-glass fly trap which resembled a fat bottle was available to kitchentenders from the early 1800s on. The onion-shaped container was filled with sugar water and corked. Just prior to a meal or when the flies became a nuisance, the trap was uncorked and set out on the dinner table or counter top. Attracted by the sweet-smelling water, the flies would enter through the small opening at the top and eventually drown in the liquid.

The Harper wire screen fly trap c. 1915. Manufactured by the Wire Goods Company of Worcester, Massachusetts.

The glass jar trap was a luxury for most households. A more affordable variety was a wire cylinder set on a wooden base made about 1880. Only about nine inches high, the trap was nothing more than a screen cone inside of a larger wire compartment. Bait was put on the wooden base and flies would enter through a small hole at the apex of the cone, never to escape. A similar 1870s model featured a quonset hut shaped top. Yet another variety, called the Harper's Patent 1875 Balloon Fly Trap, used a demispherical screen dome to catch its prey.

Long before flypaper came about, poisonous fly bait was being supplied by a number of vendors. One such product was Seiber's Magic Fly Killer, a wick type poison popular around the turn of the century. Other insect poisons, many of which were harmful to the users, were available in cans and paper sacks. Some could be bought in bulk at the local grocery store. Fly swatters could also be found in stores, but most households kept a home-made wooden splint variety around for the job.

The Improved Keyless Fly Fan, c. 1885. Manufactured by Matthai-Ingram, New York. The wind-up fan ran for 90 minutes, the calculated length of a comfortable meal in the 19th century.

Foods other than drygoods were protected by kitchen furniture built to keep out insects and, in some cases, people. Pie safes featured screen or punched tin cabinet doors which allowed baked goods to cool while keeping flies from spoiling the dessert. Most pie safes were made with key locks, presumably to keep out other hungry creatures.

When they weren't kept in an ice box, a fixture that was difficult to maintain in the summertime, meats and cheeses and other dairy products were stored in screened safes. Wire cheese domes and dish covers, available in different sizes, were used to protect food around the kitchen. Usually sold in nested sets, these 19th century devices were commonly referred to as fly screens.

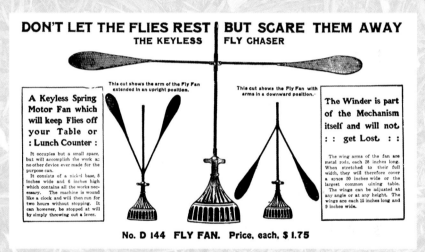

Advertisement for a clock-action fly fan, c. 1908. From the bakery supply catalog of Jaburg Brothers Co., New York.

While fly traps and screens were most common, more elaborate bug catchers and chasers were available. Although not as popular as less expensive devices, fly fans made their way into many 19th century Florida kitchens. Ingeniously made, these gadgets were powered by clockwork wind-up action. Muslin wings or small paddles would rotate from a cast iron base over food. The constant movement of the fan would distract flies and other insects, keeping them from lighting on that evening's dinner.

An 1885 model made by the National Enameling & Stamping Company advertised that the wings of its fan would rotate at least 75 minutes per wind. It was about 30″ high. Another variety, The Improved

Keyless Fly Fan (A Great Home Comfort), was made about the same time by the Matthai-Ingram Company. Its manufacturers boasted that the device would "drive all flies away by the shadow and movement of the wings while revolving," among other things.

Perhaps the most unusual contrivance invented for shooing bugs was a late 19th century contraption produced by James T. Cowan from Boston. The device was an elaborate fly fan powered by the rocking motion of a specially designed chair. Supposedly, the owner of the chair would rock comfortably while fans above kept insects away. No one is sure of how many of these "bug rockers" were actually sold.

While many things will inevitably change in their home state, Florida residents will always be guaranteed of an ample bug supply and enduringly hot summers. But we should take great comfort in knowing that the ubiquitous heat and pestilence, as much a part of the Florida experience as Disneyworld and sunny beaches, will assure us of yet another line of new-and-improved gizmos and gadgets, all devised to spare us from the little miseries in Florida living.

James T. Cowan's patented fly fan rocking chair, c. 1890s.

A Cracker homestead with a surrounding split rail fence in Eustis, c. 1892. Photograph, Florida State Archives. Gift of the Lake County Historical Association.

Houses were commonly built on elevated knolls and under enormous shade trees for maximum cooling. Shade from the large trees alone could lower the temperature of a house substantially. In some areas of the state, Cracker houses traditionally faced to the east so that residents could take advantage of eastern breezes. Ron Haase writes that there were other benefits to aligning houses in this manner: "Cracker homesteaders by and large oriented their houses on a north-south axis. It appears that this 90-degree rotation from today's best thinking had to do with maximizing the solar impact on all three sunny sides: east, south and west. Such a tactic helped to keep the log walls dry. Moisture, leading to premature decay in wood, was the worst culprit in making a home unlivable. Placement of the fireplace and chimney in the north gable end would help keep that fourth sunless wall dry as well."[5]

> "*Each region of our country has developed a distinctive architectural style. So it is with the old Cracker homesteads of Florida, whose sagging porches and rusting roofs are eloquent testimonials to a lifestyle that responded to its environment rather than fighting it.*"
>
> — FROM *CLASSIC CRACKER*,
> RONALD W. HAASE, 1992.

Original Cracker houses are rapidly disappearing from the Florida landscape. This old Cracker home, dating from the 1880s, still stands off Maytown Road between Osteen and Oak Hill, Florida. The house, with its original clapboard wood siding, shake roof (covered with tin around the turn-of-the-century), and breezeway, was built by Henry S. Clark for his family, according to Henry Clark, the great-grandson of Henry S. Clark. Henry's grandfather Arthur and his father's brother Albert also lived in the house at separate times in the early 1900s. An early outhouse still stands out back. Photograph by Dana Ste.Claire, 1996.

"Who does not know the dreary flat-woods villages of the South, with their decaying log cabins and hopelessly unfinished frame houses"

— LOUISE SEYMOUR
HOUGHTON,
*EKONIAH SCRUB: AMONG
FLORIDA LAKES,* 1880.

An abandoned red-painted Cracker house on Tahota Street in Micanopy, Florida. This house was located during a futile two-hour search for the Clyde Sutton residence featured on the cover of Ron Haase's Classic Cracker (Pineapple Press 1992, cover and p. 68) Onetime neighbor of Clyde Sutton and lifelong Micanopy resident Rutha Lee Jones emerged from her nearby house to solve the mystery of the elusive Sutton residence. When asked the whereabouts of the house, Mrs. Jones explained while chewing tobacco, "Son, you can look for that old house for the rest of your life, but you ain't never gonna find it ... that house done burnt down last year." And for emphasis, she spit and laughed out loud. She went back into her house when I asked permission to take her picture. Photograph by Roger Simms, 1997.

A forgotten Cracker home in Astor, Florida off State Road 40. Photograph by Roger Simms, 1997.

A shotgun house in DeLeon Springs, Florida. Photograph by Roger Simms, 1997.

An early Cracker house, now abandoned, in Homosassa, Florida. Photograph by Jean Hartline, 1997.

"Crackers do not often care to live in settlements or villages; instead, each small household dwells in a cabin that stands quite apart; it is built generally on a little spot in the woods, which as been cleared by toil that was almost as slow and patient, and as without feeling or interest, as a force in Nature ... The roof of their cabin is apt to be crumbled and broken; the shingles are curled and warped under cushions of green moss, and along the eaves, during the rainy season, they are almost hidden by the soft growth of tree-ferns ... The walls are logs, the spaces between them being plastered with mud; there is often no window; instead, the door stands open, letting

A primitive Cracker residence near the headwaters of the Ocklawaha River. From Florida Fancies *by F. R. Swift, 1903, p. 51.*

a square of sunshine fall upon the earthen floor (which is) higher in the centre, so that the rain dripping from the broken roof may not stand in pools about the feet; ... The chimney is on the outside of the house, and is built of mud, and girdled by barrel hoops or ropes which were put around it to support it while the mud was wet; but as the fires within dry it, it is apt to lean away from the wall of the house."

— MARGARET DELAND IN *FLORIDA DAYS*, 1889, PROVIDES THIS ACCOUNT OF CRACKER SETTLEMENT AND STYLE OF ARCHITECTURE.

Archer's log cabin in Daytona Beach, Florida c. 1875. The cabin was once located at 154 South Beach Street on land now occupied by Dunn Brothers Hardware. The Single-Pen or single-room house was usually the first construction effort of Cracker homesteaders. The simple one-room structures were built of logs, roofed with cedar shake shingles and elevated on wooden piers. Rarely did the windows have glass or screen. The Florida variant of the Single-Pen included a front porch to provide shade at the hottest times of the day. Photograph, Florida State Archives.

19th century Cracker dwelling in North Florida. Photograph, Florida State Archives.

"I remember going over to great uncle's house just across the river over in Lake County to visit him when I was a little boy. The house was built way up off the ground, it had it boarded up under there with slat boards so they keep the hogs under there and that's where the hogs stayed underneath the house and that was a good pen for 'em cause the bears would raid them and they'd keep them away."
— BILL DREGGORS, DELAND, 1996.

Houses were usually built off the ground on wedge-shaped piers of heart pine or cypress to allow circulation under the floor, for protection from standing water, and to keep the snakes and termites out. Mosquitos and horseflies were a different matter as the screenless windows of houses in Florida offered a paradise for these pests. Occasionally, windows were covered with burlap or cloth, but even then the bugs found their way in.

The few interior furnishings present were as homemade as the houses themselves. Tables and chairs were hand-fashioned out of local woods. Dried rawhide and woven cane were used as seats in chairs and Spanish moss and corn shucks were stuffed to make mattresses. Near by, an old pole and cypress knee bucket was always ready to draw water and gourds provided the necessary dippers for household use. The rustic architecture and contents of Cracker houses reflect the simple lifestyles of rural Florida settlers.

"We lived in a house like this ... full of holes. You could see the sun rise and the moon and the stars."

— PIERSON RESIDENT LUELLA ROSS DESCRIBING HER 1920S CHILDHOOD LIFE IN A THREE-ROOM SHOTGUN HOUSE. *DAYTONA BEACH NEWS-JOURNAL* ARTICLE, "TURPENTINE HOUSE ADDS CHAPTER AT SETTLEMENT," BY MELISSA KOSSLER, OCTOBER 8, 1997.

SUGGESTED READING

Ronald W. Haase, *Classic Cracker: Florida's Wood-Frame Vernacular Architecture,* Sarasota: Pineapple Press, Inc., 1992.

NOTES

1. Achille Murat, *The United States of North America* (London) 1833, p. 53.

2. Marjorie Kinnan Rawlings, *Cross Creek,* 1942, pp.74 - 75.

3. Charles W. Pierce, *Pioneer Life in Southeast Florida.* Coral Gables: University of Miami Press, 1970, p. 54.

4. Storm L. Richards, "Adaptive Features of "Cracker" Housing in North-Central Florida." *The Florida Geographer* 14, 1980, p.22.

5. Ronald W. Haase, *Classic Cracker: Florida's Wood-Frame Vernacular Architecture,* 1992, p. 42.

A late 19th century Cracker kitchen in Melrose, Florida. Photograph, Florida State Archives.

Grits and Gravy: Cracker Cuisine

"God, we thank you for all the food we got, especially the grits"

— CRACKER PRAYER. CARL ALLEN, *ROOT HOG OR DIE POOR*.

Cracker fare has endured for centuries because it provided a tasty and affordable staple to rural Southerners who got by with little or no money. There was a time when early Cracker settlers had to eat everything they could get their hands on to survive in the Florida wilds. Here, the simple diet of backwoods Floridians was created of necessity, for few settlers could afford "store-boughten" food, even if it was available to them - most had to make do with what they could find around them. Indeed, some of the greatest Cracker fare known was born out of poverty.

Few Crackers could afford "store-boughten" goods, or items available at a country store, even if there was such a place in the area. When Crackers did have a little money from the sale of moonshine, livestock, produce or hides and pelts, it was usually spent on tobacco, sugar, coffee, flour, ammunition and "store" whiskey. Fancier items like cloths and "city stuff" were just for lookin'. Store interior facade from The Cracker Culture in Florida History exhibit, Old St. Augustine Village, Museum of Arts and Sciences. Photograph, Roger Simms, 1997.

In early Florida times, you could expect to see one of the three "g's" on your supper plate - grits, greens, and gravy. Throw in a little cornbread and you have the basic and age-old food staples of Florida Crackers. Another early Cracker menu item was the "scrub chicken" or gopher tortoise, a slow moving and tasty treat for the Cracker stew. Relations of the gopher in nearby lakes and rivers ended up in the cooking pot, as well. Soft-shelled turtles called "cooter" were gathered regularly for the dinner table. While they were in the neighborhood, Cracker fishermen collected catfish, crayfish, frogs and snails. Alligators were there, too, but even the poorest Crackers rarely ate these reptiles, although the meat has become popular in recent years.

Folklore has it that all of these items, when cooked properly, tasted like chicken, which was fine with Crackers for poultry was a delicacy. When fowl was available, it was usually a Guinea

An Alligator snapping turtle, a sought after Cracker dish.

Fred Harding with a sizable rattlesnake catch, Crows Bluff, Lake County, Florida, c. 1900. From the collection of Bill Dreggors, DeLand.

hen or two, those nearly wild imports from Africa. They required little care and adapted well to the harsh backwoods landscape. As hardy stock, these birds rarely came across the table tender, and usually tasted like they "ran all the way from the border," as Cracker oldtimers

will tell you. A chicken or Guinea fowl could be stretched for days to satisfy a large family with rice, about the only grain which was stocked in the cupboard.

A Tail of Two Possums

One of the most peculiar Cracker dishes I caught wind of is a stew made with the tails of two possums, though no one seems to know why the recipe calls for a set of the appendages when one would surely do. Perhaps a long-lost Cracker superstition has something to do with it. Ernest Matthew Mickler in his *White Trash Cooking* tells us how to prepare just one of the creatures, tail and all, in two recipes called Mama Leila's Hand-Me-Down Baked Possum and Aunt Donnah's Roast Possum: "After you kill the possum be careful not to let him get away. While you're talking and planning how you going to eat him, he's going to be slipping right from under your nose. All he was doing was playing possum ... Possum should be cleaned as soon as possible after shooting ... Skin him and clean him before you go another foot, then the mess is gone and he won't get away. When you get him home, rub salt and pepper all over his body then run a mixture of vinegar and brown sugar over the salt and pepper. Wrap up the possum in a good baking pan and let it stand in the refrigerator overnight. The next morning put the pan with the possum still in it (hopefully) on top of the stove ... Possum is tender and mild regardless of what other people think ... There's only one thing to serve possum with - sweet potatoes (and) you only eat possum in the winter."

A Florida 'possum.

Gravy could stretch the pantry, too. Real Cracker gravy was grease made during the frying of fatback bacon. It was collected in a bowl and poured over grits, biscuits, sweet potatoes, and many other things. Marjorie Kinnan Rawlings in *Cross Creek* (1942) was amazed at the popular use of solid grease as a gravy, and wondered why anyone would find it palatable: "... how country stomachs survive ten hundred and ninety-five servings of this a year is a mystery past my solving."

By far, the most common Cracker food was home-ground cornmeal which could be used to beef-up the leanest of meals. Cornbread alone was often served as a meal, along with a lot of gravy, or a little sugar cane syrup, or maybe a side of homegrown sweet potatoes. Cornpone, usually fried, was made without expensive ingredients like milk and eggs.

> "I guess we had a good time eating venison back in the old days and gophers, plenty of whooping cranes. They were good to eat also. Grits was about five dollars a barrel and venison seven cent a pound and bacon about seven cents a pound. We never saw any ready ground coffee. We beat it up in a sack or tin can with a marlin spike. Could not get a coffee mill, only once in a while. Made plenty of sweet potatoes and cassava and some vegetables on the place. There was plenty of coonty roots you could grind up and make starch that make good eating. We used to grate the cassava and make starch of it."
>
> — C. S. "TED" SMALLWOOD ON CRACKER FARE IN 19TH CENTURY SOUTHWEST FLORIDA. IN CHARLTON W. TEBEAU'S *THE STORY OF THE CHOKOLOSKEE BAY COUNTRY WITH THE REMINISCENCES OF PIONEER C. S. "TED" SMALLWOOD*, 1955.

Marjorie Kinnan Rawlings offers these gradations of cornbread: "True cornbread is made elegantly with milk and eggs and shortening and is considered, rightly, good enough for any one. Then comes cornpone. It is not so rich, leaving out the eggs and usually the milk, and is made in a skillet on top of the stove. Below cornpone is hoecake and this is made simply of cornmeal, salt and water, very thin in texture, and fried in a skillet if one has fat for frying, or often in a Dutch oven or over a hearth or camp fire."[1] Cornpone, similar to the

> "Salt-beef fried in tallow and the tallow was as hard as candles ready for burning, a dish of hominy, cornbread made without salt, and coffee without milk, you can guess how much I ate."
>
> — NORTHERNER KATE HART DESCRIBING HER CRACKER BREAKFAST AT A HERNANDO COUNTY, FLORIDA BOARDING HOUSE, 1852.

Affordable staples like cornmeal sometimes provided the only food for Cracker families during lean times. Photograph, Florida State Archives.

northern "Johnny Cake," was handy because it could be cooked up in a hurry on a hot griddle and because other things could be added to the batter. Author Patrick Smith once told me that when he was younger his mother used to mix in coquina broth to flavor breakfast pone. Grits, another grade of ground corn, were standard fare, as well, and sometimes taken three times a day.

Crackling, the crisp residue left from making home-made lard, was added to breads and other foods as a special treat. The hog fat was fried and mixed into meal to make "cracklin cornbread." This delicacy usually coincided with the autumn hog-killing season. Tough fat pork or bacon, dried during butchering, was sometimes the only meat other than game available, and was sometimes served for every meal.

The Mystery of Grits

Grits, plain and simple, are pure Cracker fare, the "staff of life" of the Deep South, yet they remain as one of the most misunderstood foodstuffs to ever grace a supper table. With definitions like "ground hominy with the germ removed" (Webster's Dictionary), it is evident that even the American lexicologists are confused about this mysterious foodstuff. Just the mere name of this widely-known Southern institution has dissuaded countless people from sampling this tasty dish, one which is always served in place of potatoes, never as a cereal.

Now, for the sake of Cracker clarity, grits are not grains like wheat and rice which are taken from the stalk. Grits are ground from dried corn which was shucked and shelled from the field or bought from the store by the bag. Crackers usually grew, dried, husked and ground their own.

REG.U.S.   PAT.OFF.

NO   GRIT

The Quaker Oats Company
MANUFACTURERS & DISTRIBUTORS
ADDRESS CHICAGO, U. S. A.

An early 20th century 100lb grits cloth sack. Some Cracker oldtimer say that grits probably caused the South to lose the Civil War in that the Confederate soldiers had trouble digesting his crudely ground corn, or because they had to stop and cook a pot too often.

To make grits, whole kernels of dried corn were crushed in a cast-iron grinder or, when these were unavailable, a mortar and pestle, or just a hard stone. Sometimes, Crackers took their home-grown corn to a local grits mill to be processed. Here, large stone wheels, usually powered by a flowing creek, ground different grades of corn. The miller would crush the corn for "shares" of the grind that he in turn would sell to the local store. Carl Allen in *Root Hog or Die Poor* recalls that his family's home-grown corn "would be shelled by an old corn sheller and then carried

(Top) Korn King No. 1 1/2 Corn Grinder manufactured by the Root-Heath Mfg. Company Plymouth, Ohio, c. 1880. (Bottom) Cornmeal sifter made of wood and wire screen, c. 1900. Corn Crackin' Grits and cornmeal are made from ground dried corn, shucked and shelled from the field or bought from the store by the bag. Crackers usually grew, dried, husked and ground their own corn. To make grits and meal, whole kernels of dried corn were crushed in a cast-iron grinder or, when these were unavailable, a mortar and pestle, or with a hard stone. After grinding, the pulverized corn, hulls and all, was sifted through screens of different sized mesh. The finest, almost powdery grind was used as cornmeal, while the courser grain was bagged as grits. The hulls and anything else left over was collected for chicken feed. Long ago, grits were everything that came out of the grinder, hulls and all.
Photographs by Roger Simms, 1997.

over to the grits mill located on the northwest side of Lakeland." Just about every community in early 20th century Florida had a grits mill within a day's travel time.

A home grinder could be set in such a way that the coarseness of the crushed corn could be regulated, producing grits or meal, which ever was desired. Another technique for sorting the grind was the use of sieves. After grinding, the pulverized corn was sifted through screens of different sized mesh. The finest, almost powdery grind was used as cornmeal, while the courser grain was bagged as grits. The chaff and anything else left over was collected for chicken feed. Long ago, grits were everything that came out of the grinder, hulls and all.

The culinary institution of crushed-corn victuals seems to have been weighted by the term "hominy grits." It is unclear when these two words came together and why, as hominy and grits are two different things altogether and, according to many Cracker purists, should not be mentioned in the same breath. The dish "hominy" is whole grains of corn soaked in a mild lye solution for food. It was typically prepared this way: dry white corn was soaked overnight in a stoneware crock filled with water and a couple of tablespoons of Red Devil lye. The following day, the corn was removed and boiled in freshwater until the skins and eyes of the bloated kernels washed off. The resulting tender corn was then cooked in a cast iron pot with fatback, black pepper and and a little salt, and served "as is."

"Grits were a gift from heaven to the old folks when I was growing up, for they would cook them real mushy so they could be eaten even if one didn't have many teeth left."
— CARL ALLEN, *ROOT HOG OR DIE POOR.*

"Hominy grits," it appears, is just a regional term for pure ground-corn grits. A representative from Quaker Oaks of Chicago, Illinois acknowledged this, claiming there is no difference between the company's plain white grits and hominy grits - both are made from the same dried and ground white corn. They did mention, however, that lye was used long ago to bleach out their white grits, but this happened after the grits were ground from dried corn. Cooking guides, especially those produced in the North, often use "grits" and "hominy" interchangeably to describe grits. But there are some who have come to believe that hominy grits are in fact ground hominy corn, which begs the question: why would someone lye-soak corn to make hominy, and then take the time to redry it so that it could be ground when this could have been done in the first place? Maybe this process improved the texture and taste of the grits. Perhaps it is just a misunderstanding. So, while recognizing that redried and ground hominy may have been produced somewhere in the world at some time, and may still be, it would be derelict not to mention as a parting shot that most Crackers laugh at the whole idea of this. To them, grits are grits, ground straight from the grinder ... always has been, always will be.

Greens were important Cracker vittles, too. These days, Cracker greens mean collards, mustards and turnips. Back then, it was any plant that was edible, from wild onions to pokeweed, which was picked to make "poke salat." A convenient plant food was the heart of palm, or swamp cabbage, as Sabal Palm could be easily found in the swampy terrain around most Cracker settlements. The edible part of the palm is found in its core from the new shoots down as far as four feet in a large tree. The bud can be eaten raw, but frequently was cooked into a dish called "cabbage." The best trees, according to Cracker lore, were eight to ten feet tall and not growing too close to the water.

Coonties and Cattails:
Cracker Cookin' with Native Plants

Early Florida Crackers, like their Native Americans predecessors, used their rich natural surroundings as a backyard supermarket of sorts. While crops and game made up most of the Cracker's diet, native plants supplemented their food and guaranteed their survival during leaner times.

Plants were also used for making just about everything imaginable, from clothing to medicine, and shelters to fishing nets. Some were prevalent in everyday use, like the lowly palmetto. Found just about everywhere in Florida, it was used to thatch huts, weave mats, hats and baskets, and to fuel fires. The fiber found around the base of this plant was important for fire tender, making clothing, and for starting baskets, a technique which is still used today. The dark, olive-shaped berries of the palmetto were used by Crackers for both food and medicine, but for food only when times were desperate. The taste was described by late 1600s Florida castaway Jonathan Dickinson as something resembling rotten cheese combined with tobacco juice.

If rope was not available, thin strands of bear grass, a type of yucca, could be woven into durable cordage. Bear grass rope is one of the strongest natural lashings available in the Florida environment.

But plants served a greater role to Crackers as food and medicine. Many of these early recipes and herbal concoctions are lost forever, but we still have a good idea from historical accounts of some of the plants Crackers collected and processed into usable foods and remedies. For example, Crackers called the Hercules club the "tooth-ache tree" because when the tree's leaves were crushed and placed between the gum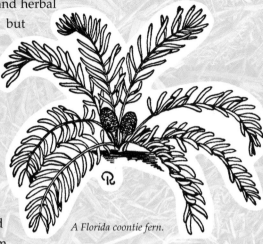

A Florida coontie fern.

and ailing tooth, it numbed the pain. Another type of folk medicine was the poultice, a medicinal salves made with plants combined with things such as soap, fat meat, chewing tobacco, chopped onion, scraped Irish potato, and wet baking soda.

Crackers learned how to eat some of the most unlikely and seemingly unappetizing plants, such as the Florida prickly pear, a spiny cactus that wards off potential pickers with some convincing weaponry. Both the plant and its reddish fruit, called "pears," were carefully deneedled, boiled and turned into an edible, but not always palatable, mash. However, the fruit of the cactus makes a tasty jelly.

Another unlikely plant food was extracted from the coontie, an unusual-looking fern-like plant which is deadly poisonous unless prepared properly. The final product was a rich starch, which must have been a highly pretty important foodstuff for settlers given the risky process involved in making it consumable.

Coontie ferns have flourished in the state for thousands of years. Despite its popular name, the unusual-looking plant is not a fern, although its feather-like, evergreen leaves give the impression of one. Also known as Florida Arrowroot, the native plant bears the state's name in its Latin description - Zamia floridana. The plant is remarkably well suited to Florida's sandy soils and highly tolerant to drought.

Historically, the coontie has served as one of the most important foods of Crackers. It was used by early settlers as a substitute for the wheat flour which they had grown accustomed to in their northern homelands. But the coontie is filled with poison which had to be carefully removed. If the starch, made from the crushed tap roots of the plant, is not allowed to ferment for some time, it will retain its hydrocyanic acid, a highly poisonous cyanide solution. Surely many early Florida settlers discovered the dangers of the plant the hard way before being shown the secret of processing the plant as an edible substance.

The method of processing the coontie fern root into starch was far from complicated, although necessarily slow and tedious. The mashed pulp of the coontie root was soaked in water and strained through skins or cloth to separate the starch from the plant. After days of fermentation in a treated solution, the coontie flour was dried in the sun, then collected for use.

The roots of aquatic plants, as well as those from upland varieties, were taken as food when available. The cattail, for example, was used in a variety of ways. From its submerged roots to its flowering tail-like tip, the cattail was a veritable food source for early settlers. The submerged tap roots of this plant were pounded and dried into a starch-like substance. During the spring, the rich pollen of cattail flowers was collected and used as a flour. Even the early green buds of cattails were collected, boiled as a tasty "corn-on-the-cob" dish.

Hickory nuts and acorns from oaks were gathered in the fall and prepared by crushing the pulp and soaking the mash to remove impurities. The nutmeat of the Pignut hickory was added to muffins and ground into a meal which was used to thicken soups and stews. By boiling hickory nut mash, a butter-like oil was produced which was used to supplement other foods. After soaking the tannic acid from acorns, the meats were ground into usable flour.

Berries were usually gathered during the spring and summer. When a berry harvest was plentiful, the surplus was sometimes canned and stored as food for the lean months. Blueberries, blackberries, huckleberries, elderberries, mulberries, wild grapes, black cherries and plums were just some of the fruits taken seasonally by Cracker settlers. Many of the berries, like elderberries, were used to make fruity wines.

The signature Cracker pilau is almost a sacred dish, and for making a small amount of meat feed a large number of people, it has no equal. A pilau is any dish of meat and rice cooked together, like a chicken pilau, or squirrel or pork, or even a Minorcan seafood pilau.[2] The word is pronounced "per-loo" and sometimes spelled "perleu" by Crackers. John Y. Willis, Sr. of Custom Cracker Cookouts spells his "purlo" phonetically just to avoid the confusion. He explains that the old-time pilau was created to use up old hens, or those chickens which didn't "lay enough eggs to justify their feed." The recipe is simple: simmer chicken or fresh pork, or any other type of meat in a pot of water, and when the meat begins to fall from the bones, add enough rice to feed everyone who showed up for dinner. But John cautions that a good pilau has to be cooked carefully. Back when the dish was prepared outside, slow fuel like palmetto roots and other soft woods were stacked and burned around a large cast iron pot, allowing the chicken to steam for three to four hours. Fat pine was forbidden, as it made a fire too hot to cook pilau the right way. And there are other culinary taboos, too, like adding peas and carrots, which, according to John, made a pilau something else, like "chicken and rice." The pilau rightly should not be called this, but if it is, it should be referred to as a "Sunday go-to-meetin' chicken and rice," as John's grandmother explained long ago.

Things that couldn't go in a pilau were prepared in other ways. Somewhere in the history of Cracker cooking, rattlesnakes became an entree, probably when the creatures came too close to the homestead. It is a very boney dish and requires a fat snake for a full meal. Cracker cook Euda M. Alderman of Oak Hill explains that any rattler under six foot is just a waste of time. When cooked the right way, the meat tastes similar to chicken (of course) or frog legs. Allen's Historical Cafe in Auburndale, Florida suggests freezing the rattlesnake overnight before cooking it and, most important, removing enough of the poisonous end of the snake to make sure that the dish doesn't become your last meal. Armadillos, after they were introduced to Florida in the earlier part of this century, became a fairly regular Cracker dish. Sometimes referred to as "swamp pork,"

Rattlesnake is a Cracker delicacy, but one which has to be prepared carefully.

armadillo was prepared by marinating the shelled animal in vinegar or garlic water and deep frying it. Dark in color, it too tastes like chicken.

In the leanest of times, the Cracker simply learned to make do. Game meat and fish were preserved with salt from the roots of saw palmettos when it was impossible to get salt from the coast. If coffee was unavailable or unaffordable, Crackers roasted field corn until it was dark brown and almost burnt, crushed it, and used it for grounds. Employing an age-old Native American process, the settlers substituted dried cootie fern or cattail root for flour, and wild honey replaced sugar.

Florida swamp pork, the ubiquitous armadillo.

As the Cracker folk will tell you, the Cracker kitchen "never stopped cooking," at least during the cooler seasons. To beat the mid-day summer heat, Cracker women would rise well

"If it walked, and didn't talk, we ate it"

— MILLARD ZUBER ON THE SELECTIVE NATURE OF CRACKER MENUS, NOVEMBER 1990.

before dawn, sometimes as early as 3 a.m., to cook bread, biscuits and meats for the rest of the day, as hearths or wood stoves in a closed kitchen were insufferable. A hot breakfast was served at the accustomed sunrise hour, then everything cooked that morning was placed in the middle of the table and covered by folding the corners of a table cloth over the food, which required little effort to warm up at later times of the day. Marjorie Kinnan Rawlings observed this style of preparation at many Cross Creek households: "It was only as I came to know the backwoods cooking customs that I knew that enough food was cooked once or at the most twice a day, to last for the three meals. The people were up long before daylight and the remnants of the

"Crackers prefer to cook out of doors, and so, near the cabin, a fire is built between three great stones, which serve as a tripod for their kettles, and a thin twist of blue smoke as straight as a staff rises into the still air."

— MARGARET DELAND, *FLORIDA DAYS*, 1889.

previous evening's biscuits and greens and fat bacon were set aside for the early breakfast, eaten by lamplight."[3] A typical early morning breakfast of cornpone, fat back, and muddy, pitch black coffee. And then something was always on the

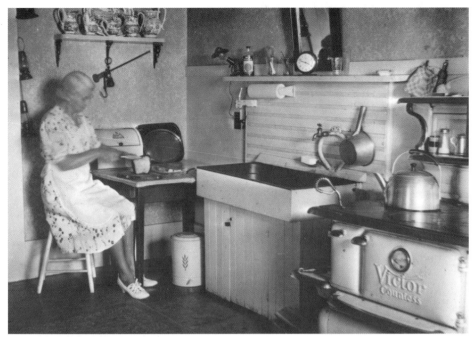

The kitchens changed, but the food stayed the same. An "upscale" Cracker kitchen of the Breen home, Pensacola, Florida. Photograph, Florida State Archives.

back of the stove for the night's supper, like a pot of possum and dumplings ... and grits, of course.

Southern cuisine is served in restaurants throughout Florida, but the truth is that good traditional Cracker foods, the staple of the deep South, are hard to find, even in restaurants that advertise home-cooked Southern fare. This should come as a surprise to all

> *"It was dark when Tobias hung the last section of meat in the smokehouse and stoked the fire. Every ounce of the bull would be used. The tail was skinned and chopped into sections for stew, and the leg bones and ribs would go to soup. The brains would be scooped out and fried, and the hooves boiled into jelly. Tobias would take the hide and horns to the settlement. He thought he would get at least two dollars in trade for the hide. Emma smiled and said, 'In the morning I'll boil the heart and liver for breakfast.'"*
>
> — PATRICK SMITH, *A LAND REMEMBERED*, 1984.

Southern folk because this is the very culinary foundation on which most country cooking was built.

Moonshining

"The old man makes very good shine, so they say, and now and then does a little fishing and gator hunting. He drinks a pint and a half of whiskey every day, and will tell you all about his still except for where it is."
— ANONYMOUS EARLY 1900S FORKED RIVER DREDGE HAND QUOTED IN LAWRENCE WILL'S *CRACKER HISTORY OF OKEECHOBEE*, 1964.

Next to truck farming, moonshining was one of the most lucrative enterprises of rural Cracker settlers, although most won't admit to doing it. Moonshine, or "low bush lightning" as it was called in the backcountry, is distilled corn whiskey, usually made in a large, hand-fashioned copper still.

To make "shine," dried corn or whole-grain rye mixed with water - a concoction called "mash" - was allowed to soak and ferment in a fifty-gallon lidded barrel for two or three days in the summer, and up to a week in the winter. After the grain fermented, a large amount of sugar, usually about fifty pounds, was added to it. The chemical reaction released heat and made the mixture "boil" for several days. When the batch stopped cooking, the "soured" water, called "rubin" in some areas and "buck" in others, ladled off was cooked in a still.

Steam from the boiled mixture would rise to the top of the still and pass through a long copper coil. The alcohol condensation which formed

A copper moonshine still at the Pioneer Settlement for the Creative Arts, Barberville, Florida. Photograph by Roger Simms, 1997.

A moonshine still near Tampa during a revenuer raid, c. 1920. Photograph, Florida State Archives.

in the copper worm slowly dripped out of the pipe into a "catch," or any type of container, such as a Mason jar, stoneware jug, or for larger quantities, a barrel. The coil was usually submerged in cold water to accelerate the process of condensation. To make an extra potent batch of "shine," the collected alcohol was "run back through" or double distilled.

The long process would net little more than five gallons of moonshine, but the 98% to 100% proof liquor was hard to come by, so it could be sold for a premium price. The expensive "shine" was that which wasn't sold off right away, but instead allowed to age in an oak barrel for several months, sometimes with charred peaches to give the whiskey a pleasant and distinguishing blush color and eliminate the bitter taste. In the 1930s, the "good stuff" might sell for fifty or sixty dollars for a five-gallon jug.

When moonshine was illegal during the days of Prohibition, distillery operations went underground. Stills were hidden away deep in the Florida backwoods, as far away from the revenuers as possible. Moonshiners, or the owners of the distilleries, manufactured their whiskey in these remote areas and sold it to bootleggers who in turn distributed a cut and marked-up version of the "shine" to customers. For all of the parties involved, moonshining was a game, with everyone trying to outsmart the other. The law-enforcing revenuers knew most of

A revenuer destroying a moonshine still in Polk County, Florida, c. 1930s. Photograph, Florida State Archives.

the moonshiners and boot-leggers, and over and over they were caught and released with little more than a fine levied. Stricter state and federal agents, armed with axes, would destroy an entire distillery operation, causing the moonshiner to relocate and rebuild his still in a few days time. Marjorie Kinnan Rawlings in her *Cross Creek* explains the Central Florida version of the game: "That anomaly, 'Prohibition,' was still in force, and our liquor was good moonshine from the Florida scrub. We brought it almost openly, bringing it home in five-gallon glass demijohns and siphoning it off into charred oak kegs to ripen. The local sheriff was in cahoots with the moonshiners, arresting only those who did not pay his weekly tribute. A plutocrat was one who could buy 'shine enough ahead of his needs to have always a fully mature supply on hand. The riff-raff drank from hand to mouth of improperly aged liquor, and it was a mark of caste to serve one's 'corn' not less than six or eight months old. I managed to put by two five-gallon kegs, for it was enough for friends to drive twenty-five miles to call on me, without offering them raw liquor."

Michel Oesterreicher's *Pioneer Family: Life on Florida's 20th-Century*

Copper moonshine still with brass fittings, c. 1895. From the collection of Dave and Gloria Burnell, Museum of Yesteryear, New Smyrna Beach, Florida. Small stills like this one were used to process a few gallons of whiskey for family consumption. Photograph by Roger Simms, 1997.

Frontier recounts the 1932 moonshining activities of her grandfather Hugie Oesterreicher and the difficulties involved in running a still during Prohibition. When federal agents started cracking down on huge orders of sugar by staking out wholesale warehouses throughout Florida, Hugie and his wife Oleta were forced to traveled from store to store in Duval and

"When someone bought four to five-hundred pounds of sugar, it was a sure bet that it wasn't for jelly or cake"

— EAST FLORIDA CRACKER STAN TAYLOR ON SUSPECT BUYS OF MOONSHINE-MAKING SUGAR IN THE EARLY 1900S. IN ANN TAYLOR'S, *TALES OF FLORIDA CRACKERS: HISTORY, HUNTING, AND HUMOR,* 1996.

St. Johns Counties, buying five and ten pound bags here and there to collect the amount needed to make good and profitable whiskey.

Soon after Hugie paid for the delivery of his last child with moonshine money, Prohibition was repealed and what was once a lucrative business for him was over. With nothing left to do, Hugie hauled his large copper still in the back of his truck to a Jacksonville junkyard, where he sold it for scrap metal. Town folks along the streets of Jacksonville stared in disbelief at this brash Cracker as he toted his still through the busy city. But as author Oesterreicher points out, Hugie wasn't proud that he had to run moonshine to survive, and he wasn't ashamed of it either.

Corn Chatter

As the mainstay of Cracker fare and one of the simplest yet most misunderstood Cracker foodstuffs, corn - and everything made from it and everything related to it - is busy enough a topic to have its own expert commentary.

Gloria and Dave Burnell at the Marjorie Kinnan Rawlings home in Cross Creek, 1990. Photograph by Dana Ste.Claire.

So, in December of 1996, I went to Cracker cooking and corn gurus Dave and Gloria Burnell of New Smyrna Beach to help me sort out the finer points of corn crops, grits, cornmeal, cornbread, cornpone, hoecake, hominy, grits mills, and grinding ... and a few other things in between. In the interview, I am persistent in getting all of the details about growing, picking and processing corn. At times this is frustrating to Dave Burnell who knows his corn like the back of his hand and has better things to do than explain the obvious to a greenhorn. At other times, the dialogue turns humorous as routine processes and the meaning of Crackerisms are examined to the point of being comical. In the end, though, the Burnells clear up a good many things about corn and, most important, solve the great mystery of what grits are and where they come from.

Ste.Claire: Take me all the way from the very beginning on this ... I want to go from the field to the table. You were telling me about the different crops of corn and how they were used. Tell me about it, you said the first kind was used for something and the second kind for something else ...

Dave Burnell: No, what they done ... they bought the seed like the seed that comes in that seed bag in there and they then planted that in the ground and then in the fall of year when it got ripe, they husked it. A lot of places did, up north ... they husked it, shelled the corn and then they separated the corn, they graded the corn, they got the good kernels and the medium kernels and the small kernels, after they husked the corn....

Ste.Claire: And after they husked the corn? ... That was like a preliminary cut, when the corn came out, right? When they picked the corn out of the field, how would they dry it?

Burnell: Well, back when you wanted to do, it was dried in the field.

Ste.Claire: They just let it dry out on the stalk.

Burnell: Well ... and then they took it to the barn and then put it in cribs and the cribs had slats on the cracks and they'd go in there and the air could blow through there and that would finish drying it for it was pretty well dried when they took it out of the field for they didn't have no way of dryin' corn. Today they go in there with a combine and they combined it and they take it right to the mill and they'd run it to the big dryer, they dry it and that's the way it goes, you know. But back then they'd go out there, they shucked it by hand, hauled it to the barn and shoveled over into these cribs and then the air would go through there. Then as they needed corn along through the winter or the spring or whenever they was going to use the corn, well they'd take some in the barn. They had these hand-cranked corn shellers that would take the corn off the cob and they would get that a bucketful or whatever shell off and then they had a mill that they would grade it in. I got a little hand grader there at home. And they'd dump it in there and just shake this back and forth and the slots are different sizes and the little stuff kept fallin down, down, down and the big stuff would set on the top, that was the best corn, so that was either kept to make corn meal out of or grits or whatever or for planting again the next year and then the next....

Ste.Claire: The dry corn could be planted and it would germinate and become plants again.

Burnell: Become plants again, right.

Ste.Claire: So the biggest corn was selected out for either processing or replanting.

Burnell: Right.

Ste.Claire: And the second grade of corn was used for what?

Burnell: Well, they, a lot of people might even use some of that in the household, but a lot of it was used then to feed the chickens or the hogs or whatever, you know, and the further down you went the less the value of it was, you know.

Ste.Claire: Do they have a name for it like grade A, or....

Burnell: No, they just don't.

Ste.Claire: Just good corn and bad corn.

Burnell: Yeah, well, now they sell it by the size, they have large, medium and small and....

Ste.Claire: And everything else that's left over...

Burnell: Well, yeah, but used to you bought a bushel of corn, now you buy so many seeds.

Ste.Claire: I see.

Burnell: You buy like maybe eighty-eight thousand seeds in a bag you know, same way with grass seed and all that stuff. You don't buy it by the bag anymore, you buy it by the amount of seed that you're gonna get and that's the way corn is today. Used to you went to the feed mill and you bought a, like that pioneer thing there, the seed corn and you brought it home and you got...well they had what you call flats and grounds and medium and large, you know, in different sizes and then you bought a plate that fit in your planter for that size of corn that you have and then that would drop the corn out as you went down to do the planting. Then when it come up again, well, they'd shuck it. And see, used to they never bought seed every year until just the last few years, but they hybrid - what they called hybrid - all the time this stuff so much that this hybrid corn it don't come back good the second time. It's either small or something like that... That's why you got to buy new seed every year. But back, in them days like you're talkin' about, they used the same seed over they just kept the best stuff out, and another thing I got there at home that you seen, I know, is a corn drier. And they stuck ears of corn on there, they'd maybe pick out some real nice ears of corn and they would stick them on there and hang them up and save them for seed corn...

Ste.Claire: Now the third tier, the low-grade corn, what was that used for?

Burnell: That was hog feed.

Ste.Claire: Just straight hog feed.

Burnell: See they take that and grind that in with some better corn or some oats and stuff and make hog feed out of it.

Ste.Claire: Mush.

Burnell: We call it slops. And a lot of them used to take the corn and put it in fifty-five gallon drums and fill it full of water and let it soak until it got soft and then they'd just shovel that out or dump it out and they most generally fed them hogs on a slab of concrete, you know. I know at home where we had hogs at, we had a crib on each side and we'd shovel the corn right over in there and leave the pigs ... would eat it out of there and time we got rid of the pigs we'd scoop that all out and start right over again. Threw it right out of the crib, right out on the floor for them to eat it.

Ste.Claire: Now most of the rural Cracker folks ... if they grew any corn, there wasn't a lot of it.

Burnell: No.

Ste.Claire: So they were buying it pretty cheap. If they wanted to make their own grits, which probably was a lot cheaper, how would they have bought the corn at the store? They would have bought sacks of regular corn, not seed corn.....

Burnell: No, they just bought corn.

Ste.Claire: Not cracked corn?

Burnell: No, just shelled corn.

Ste.Claire: Just shelled corn. Alright.

Burnell: If they was gonna make their grits out of it and I'll tell you down here 90% of it would have been white corn for they grew white corn down here. Up north I don't know if anybody ever grew corn up there, but the yellow corn can make hominy ... you can get yellow hominy or white hominy. And they bleach that corn, they can bleach that corn till it is snowwhite if they bleach it. But down here they use a lot of ... down here they call it snap corn. The reason why, they snap the whole ear off the stalk. And then when it goes to the mill for feed, hog feed or cow feed, they grind the shuck and the cob and everything up see, but if it's gonna go for human consumption well, then they gotta shuck it and shell it and ... depending on what they use it for. Grampa Burnell ... I used to run around with him when I was just a little kid, and they'd cut that corn out of the field. They'd cut 10 hills square and shock it all together, a big shock.....

Ste.Claire: What's 10 hill, what's a hill?

Burnell: That's a hill of corn, 10 hill square. They'd cut all that and bring it into one shock and they'd take four....

Ste.Claire: A shock?

Burnell: Yeah! (impatient, but smiling)

Ste.Claire: S-H-O-C-K

Burnell: Yeah, a shock of corn.

Ste.Claire: Alright back up now, I don't want to interrupt you, but tell me what a hill is.

Burnell: That's where a kernel of corn comes off.

Ste.Claire: I see. So ten plants.

Burnell: Yeah! Ten hill square. And that would be all way around and everything in there. And they most generally take the four center ones and they would tie them together just like you were gonna have beans or something like that there. And then they would stack this corn around there. Then they put a (binder) on it and tie it up and they'd leave it out there till they got ready to use it in the fall. And that's most generally if they didn't have a corn crib to put it in. And that's where it dried at, it set there in that shock.

Ste.Claire: Why do they call it a shock?

Burnell: (not pleased that we are revisiting this topic) Well, that's what it is ... a shock of fodder. It's all put in a big circle and that's what they called it, a shock.

Ste.Claire: A shock.

Burnell: And then Grampa Burnell, well everybody done it ... they'd go out and take a wagon, a spring wagon sort of like that little wagon up there at the Museum ..... and they'd throw a couple of shocks of corn on there and they'd bring it to the barn and they'd clean it on the barn floor out of the cold or wherever, and they shuck all that out...

Ste.Claire: Throw in the husks and the stalks and all of that.

Burnell: And then load the stalks and the husks back up on the wagon and take that back out and scatter it in the pasture for the cows to eat and they'd eat a lot of it too ... A lot of them chop it up real fine and put molasses on it. But then they'd take them ears of corn and that's when they'd run it through their sheller again and get it shelled and then if they was gonna grade it to keep the seed or whatever, or make cornmeal or whatever, you know, well they'd keep the best corn out for that and the rest of it would go to chicken feed or hog feed or cow feed or whatever......

Ste.Claire: Alright ... so they grew corn if they were lucky enough to have enough land to grow crops, and if they were ambitious enough, and a lot of them were. But if they wanted cornmeal, which was the stock of all Cracker cooking ... if they wanted meal, and they didn't have planted corn, then they would go to the store and buy the shelled corn and bring that home ... or if they processed it through their own sheller, they would select out the good corn to make meal. Now take me through this process ... how they ground corn into grits with the grinder.

Burnell: Right, and that big grinder that I got down there (house) that I had up there, that's an ideal one. I'll bet that one was used in a grocery store as sure as I'm settin' here ... to grind corn. A person would come in there for five pounds grits. That old boy would shovel five pounds of corn in there, run it through there and it come out the other side ... then you shake it out and you could have one (screen) for cornmeal and one for grits and that's the way you would get that there. And then this husk that would be the tail end of it, it would be chicken feed in there, you know.

Ste.Claire: So someone could go and have that done at the store...

Burnell: In the grocery store, yeah. For if they didn't have a little thing like this here (grinder) or if they had to do it like the Indians with a bowl and a stone, for see that was the first way they done it ... and then they come out with this like that there. Now a lot of people had that little thing in their house and the old woman would say well, will you have some cornmeal, you know. Bring up some, you know. Well, he'd bring up a box of corn or whatever and she'd crank it through there, maybe she'd run it through there twice to get it a little finer, you know. That's the way that she would get the cornmeal or the grits.

Ste.Claire: So they would have different size grains of cracked corn that would come out. You said it might have been screened through a strainer on top of a box, a wooden box maybe. So that when they were cracking the corn through there it would come out and would go across different layers of screen ... have you actually seen this? Describe to me what this looked like.

Burnell: Well, that guy (Dick Anderson) come from Barberville, he got the set-up right up there.

Ste.Claire: Well, that's a big set-up. That's a pretty big set-up.

Burnell: This here would work on the same scale as ... but like that guy in the store, his was mostly all hand operated, you know. Just like a grinder. But see that thing of Dick's (Barberville demonstrator) that all falls out in this thing here and it's a shaker like this.

Ste.Claire: It's a mechanical shaker.

Burnell: Yeah!

Ste.Claire: But they would do it by hand, too.

Burnell: Right. And whatever would come through there, well, that would be your finest stuff, you know, depending on the size of it. And then you got that there done well, just like Dick's does ... the fine, well he keeps that, and the coarser that goes into the next stream and it's starts shaking it, you know, well then that goes through there and that's the grits and then what goes out the end, that's the hull ... it's chicken feed.

Ste.Claire: Alright, then it was graded. But now how did a poor Cracker person who didn't have a mechanical.....

Burnell: He never graded.

Ste.Claire: He never graded?

Burnell: No he'd probably just grind the corn, shell the corn and grind it and they'd eat it.

Ste.Claire: And that was the grits.

Burnell: Grits or the meal. Depending on how fine. They might run it through there a couple of times to make it finer for cornmeal, you know.

Ste.Claire: So they didn't have a bag of grits and a bag of cornmeal. They had a bag of corn grounds.

Burnell: The guy (Dick Anderson) there at Barberville, he does it that way. He just grinds it (everything) and puts it in a bag.

Ste.Claire: I see, so it's ground corn, husks and all.

Burnell: Guy told me up there at that Cracker breakfast, "Why I bought some of them up there at that (Barberville) mill but mine never tasted like this." "Why," I said, "you never got the right ones then. You got them from that guy down there that he puts the husk and everything in it. Whatever comes out, that's his grits and his cornmeal (combined). And where Dick's are separated," I said, "If you get the cornmeal or the grits with the husks gone out of there, you got clear good stuff, you know."

Ste.Claire: Alright, that answers an important question. So the poor folks would grind this stuff up somehow ... some of them were probably too poor to own a grinder or even have corn ground in a store. But they would get it somehow ... they'd buy it as cheaply as possible and maybe grind it up with a mortar and pestle or a stone and a rock ...

Burnell: The Indians did.

Ste.Claire: Somehow it would become ground corn and that's what is important.

Burnell: See, Harold, he's got a real good thing up there that would go good in that thing too. It's back in the Civil War he figures, that grinder I fixed for him.

Ste.Claire: Right. I saw it.

Burnell: And it is. Now that is a crude one there. And that's a deal where you grind it and you eat what comes out, you know. And he said that's why they had so much trouble with soldiers in the war, cause that corn was so course they couldn't digest it, you know, they'd die, well a lot of them died from it. They couldn't grind it fine enough to make it where it was digestible. And that's just like a animal too, a cow or a pig or anything, after that corn is shelled and dried,

if you don't crank (grind) on that corn, it will come right through that cow or pig or whatever or horse or whatever eats it. If they don't trip and break it before it gets into their stomach, they'll never digest it, it'll come right out on the board. And that's why when they started doing high-moisture corn and stuff in New York they had these burn mills and they just put that, run that shelled corn that they brought in out of the fields into there and they just mash that enough that would separate that hull in there so that the cow would digest it and get some good out of it for if she didn't digest it she didn't get no good out of it. See, that's the reason why they had to do that. Of course a pig, they're different, they chew a lot of that up, but like I said, back there they used to put corn in a fifty-five gallon barrel and fill it full of water, you know, and let it soak and then it was soft and then it was digestible, you know they could digest it. Otherwise you couldn't.

Dick Anderson grinds grits and corn meal at the Pioneer Settlement for the Creative Arts' Fall Jamboree. Photograph by Dana Ste.Claire, 1997.

Ste.Claire: *So, going back to the store, somebody could go to a grocery store and order five pounds of grits, or even five pounds of coffee, and it would be ground.*

Burnell: *Yeah. Absolutely.*

Ste.Claire: *Now if I ordered five pounds of grits, would they put in five pound of corn into the grinder and whatever came out was what I would get, or would I actually get five pounds of pure grits? Or would it be like five pounds of coffee ... whatever came out?*

Burnell: *Right. That's what you'd get.*

Ste.Claire: *Alright so it really wasn't five pounds of ground coffee. It was more like five pounds of coffee beans.*

Burnell: *Well, coffee beans ... I think it would be awfully close after you run it* through a grinder or whatever, you know. And see another way I think they might have done that too if you wanted grits, they opened it up and then grind it as coarse, and if you wanted cornmeal, then they screwed them things in so they're tighter, so it ground a little finer. See, I don't think most of them stores had a grinder like you got down there at my place. They just ground whatever they wanted.....

Ste.Claire: So you don't think they were sifting at the grocery store?

Burnell: Not that much.

Ste.Claire: Now assuming somebody wanted to do this the right way and separate the two ... they could sift to get grits and then sift that grade in a finer screen to get cornmeal.

Burnell: You would go buy the cornmeal. And that would keep your grits up there yet. Then you'd dump it over into another one a little bit coarser and then you get your grits, and then what would be left in there would be the husk.

Ste.Claire: Oh, I see, so you dump it all in the fine screen first ... you get the cornmeal out of there first. Then you go to a slightly coarser screen to get the grits and then you end up with ...

Burnell: Whatever is left in there.

Ste.Claire: Which is called what?

Burnell: Hulls.

Ste.Claire: And, again, that would have been used for what?

Burnell: Chicken feed or hog feed. There'd be a little bit of corn in it too.

Ste.Claire: So I end up with a sack of cornmeal and a sack of grits. Making grits is relatively easy. You take the grits, you boil them....

Burnell: With two cups of water to one cup of grits.

Ste.Claire: And then you add butter or bacon fat, whatever you wanted to add to it.

Burnell: Salt.

Ste.Claire: Alright, now the cornmeal. Tell me how to make corn pone. Is corn pone the same thing as johnny cake?

Burnell: Yeah, just different places have different names for it.

Ste.Claire: Alright, tell me about corn pone.

Burnell: Corn pone is just a cornmeal that's mixed up most generally with an egg, and.... two cups of milk and a cup of cornmeal mixed and beat up together and you fry it.

Ste.Claire: Yeah, could you make it with cornmeal and water?

Burnell: Yeah. I guess you could.

Ste.Claire: The poor folk probably had to do it that way. Alright, now what's hominy?

Burnell: Hominy is corn that's just bubbled up. I don't know how it's done in the mill but it's just a white kernel of corn is all it is.

Ste.Claire: And soaked.

Burnell: But you can get hominy yellow, too. Up north in Indiana, a lot of hominy is yellow. But you can get it white, and yellow corn would be bleached out. Yeah, it's soaked and swelled up someway but it's just a kernel of corn that's never been cracked or... it just swelled up.

Ste.Claire: What do you do with it?

Burnell: You eat it.

Ste.Claire: Just like that?

Burnell: Yeah, they can it. Didn't you ever buy hominy in the store?

Ste.Claire: No. I'm from Ocala and I never had anything like that. I knew what it was but I thought it had a bitter taste.

Burnell: No, No...

Ste.Claire: So what's the difference between that and canned corn?

Burnell: Well a canned corn is just the corn off the cob and this hominy it's blowed up and it's a round. We'll have to get a can of that and you'll have to try it. But I like it. We eat a lot of it in Indiana. You don't even see it down here for they don't have it down here like they do up there. You know it's a different part of the country and have different things, but that's the way hominy was fixed.

Ste.Claire: You make corn bread with cornmeal or with grits?

Burnell: With cornmeal. Fine meal.

Ste.Claire: Fine cornmeal. And how do you make that? Same way as corn pone? What's the difference between corn pone and corn bread?

5 LBS.
Fresh Ground
OLD FASHIONED

WHITE   BOLTED
MANUFACTURED BY
DILLSBORO MILLS
DILLSBORO, IND.

Cornmeal sack, c. 1930s. Museum of Arts and Sciences; gift of David and Gloria Burnell.

Burnell: *Not a hell of a lot. One you baked and the other you fried, you know.*

Ste.Claire: *OK, that's good. That's the difference.*

Burnell: *Gloria usually makes it with an egg, and I don't know, she might put one cup water, one cup milk or whatever and mix that all together and put it in a pan and bake it. Cut it out and it's corn bread. If you put it out in a little pan and you fry it, it's corn pone or johnny cakes. Hell, they got all kinds of names for it in the cookbooks in there. But I know it takes two cups of milk. And that's another thing we got up there this year. We got whole milk, cause we used* one cup of whole milk and one cup of skimmed milk, I think. Or maybe one cup of water and a egg for it put a little more in it with the whole milk than the skimmed milk..... we got about 1/2 gallon left of that. I just can't hardly drink it any more after drinking that skim milk. And it ain't no good for you anyway...... But that's just the way you work that there.

Ste.Claire: *Well, that's good. Well we've made it to the table. Gloria, what is the quickest and the cheapest way of making corn bread. I mean if I was a poor Cracker, how would I have made it?*

Gloria Burnell: *Well, grind up your own corn.*

Ste.Claire: *Get the cornmeal somehow.*

Gloria Burnell: *Yeah, if you didn't have any flour. You wouldn't even have to use flour if you didn't have any.*

Ste.Claire: *So you add flour to the cornmeal to make cornbread?*

Gloria Burnell: *Yeah, a little bit and I put eggs in it and milk. But back then they used just water.*

Ste.Claire: *Just water and cornmeal. Now would it rise very high?*

Gloria Burnell: *No. It wouldn't be as thick.*

Ste.Claire: Now if I was a poor Cracker and all I had was cornmeal or, as Dave explained to me, just ground corn with everything mixed in, and I wanted to make corn bread, it wouldn't be the tastiest thing in the world, would it? What would I add to it to make it better?

Gloria Burnell: Salt. With a little bit of salt they put in it back then. And sugar maybe.

Ste.Claire: Salt. Maybe some cane syrup on top of it for dessert.

Dave Burnell: I know they had cornmeal just about every meal.

Gloria Burnell: They ground their own flour too. So they might a put a little flour in it. Make it so it would raise.

Ste.Claire: They ground their own flour from what? From wheat?

Gloria Burnell: Wheat.

Ste.Claire: Well, that was pretty......was that expensive?

Dave Burnell: No, we had a grinder at home when I was at home around 1937. We had a little..... tractor and had a grinder set there in the barn and daddy he ground all our flour and corn meal and everything.

Gloria Burnell: They didn't have fine flour but they had wheat flour. They could make oat flour— they used it back then— out of oatmeal with oats. They'd grind wheat or oats - either one - to make flour.

Ste.Claire: If I wanted to make up a hearty meal and I had that corn bread there, what sort of thing would I add to it.

Gloria Burnell: Bean soup. Pot of bean soup.

Dave Burnell: Fatback.

Ste.Claire: Now what exactly is fatback?

Dave Burnell: That's the fat right off the back of an old hog.

Ste.Claire: It is ...?

Gloria Burnell: Before they smoke it, it's just more or less like a chunk of lard.

Ste.Claire: How would you eat it?

Gloria Burnell: Well, you just cook it in there for it would make a flavor for the beans.

Ste.Claire: So you cook it in the beans?

Gloria Burnell: Yeah, and then it would get soft to where you could cut it up *with a fork and eat..... be just square chunks of fat.*

Ste.Claire: Was fatback always off the hog or was it taken off the cow, too?

Gloria Burnell: No.

Ste.Claire: So it was like real fatty bacon.

Gloria Burnell: Like between, you know, how bacon you get the white strip along the top well that's the fatback. Only then they didn't smoke it. And they were poorer so there wasn't too much of that fat in there, but they called it fatback because it was along the back of the pig.

Ste.Claire: So I would drop it in a pot of beans. It would cook it in there. What were some other ways of using fatback?

Gloria Burnell: Well, they, some people cooked it until it was crunchy and then they'd eat it (raw) you know, like popcorn. They called it cracklin.

Ste.Claire: That's very popular today. People eat it like potato chips.

Gloria Burnell: They could also put a chunk of it in if they cooked a head of cabbage and made boiled cabbage, or you could put it in any vegetable....

Ste.Claire: Swamp cabbage.

Gloria Burnell: Yeah.

Dave Burnell: And another thing, they cooked it down to make their lard, too, and got their lard out of it.

Gloria Burnell: They strained fat with a piece of cloth ... cooked all this in a pot and strained it through a cloth to take out the kernels, and squeeze it and that was their lard they used to fry everything.

Ste.Claire: Now, they would cook what down? The fatback?

Gloria Burnell: The fatback from the pig.

Ste.Claire: Well what kernels are you talking about?

Gloria Burnell: Well the hide. The hide was on there so that would get real crunchy along the edge. When you took this and you cut it up in squares the hide would be on there and then this white fat would be there, you boil it. I usually did it in the oven but you can boil it on top the stove.

Ste.Claire: These were the kernels?

Gloria Burnell: No, they're rinds, they would call them rinds.

Ste.Claire: The rinds. I thought you were talking about corn kernels.

Gloria Burnell: No, rinds they would be called. And they float to the top and you skim those off but you still...there might be some crumbs in there...so you strain that and it would be as white as snow.

Dave Burnell: What they done, they put it in a piece of cheesecloth and then, I got some of Gloria's at home that her grandmother used to have, that you squeeze that boiling hot and you get every bit of the lard out of that fat then. And then we had what they called cracklins was what was left. And you heard about cracklin corn bread, well they grind them up and put that in their corn bread.

Ste.Claire: So that was the rind.

Dave Burnell: Yeah.

Ste.Claire: So that's cracklin corn bread.

Gloria/Dave Burnell: Yeah.

Ste.Claire: You would actually put that in the cornmeal.

Gloria Burnell: Yeah, with cornmeal and bake it. That made it richer because there's some of that lard there. I always made pie dough, with lard. I never did use Crisco till the last few years. I always had lard.

Dave Burnell: We had five gallon jugs there at home. In five gallon cans, I know we had seven or eight of them every winter, every fall.

Ste.Claire: What else would you use lard for?

Gloria Burnell: Fry your eggs in, in the morning, your fried potatoes and you put a spoonful in it in just about every vegetable you cook because you didn't have...unless you had a cow and made your own butter.

Dave Burnell: But a lot, I don't think they use it as much any more for if they fry any bacon they got enough grease on that. The way I always like my eggs fixed is fry them in bacon have about that much grease and put an egg in there and put that grease up over to to get the yolk to where it wasn't done, but it was covered....

Gloria Burnell: Make the top turn white instead of turning it over.

Ste.Claire: You can't have those anymore.

Dave Burnell: No.

Gloria Burnell: There's 230 grams of cholesterol in a egg yolk.

Ste.Claire: You can think about those eggs in your daydreams now.

Dave Burnell: Yeah. You got that right.

Gloria Burnell: Now, we had our own pigs. When him and I were on the farm we still raised our own pigs and I cooked that lard down when we butchered a pig and I never did buy any Crisco. I always used the lard for the pie dough. It makes a real flaky pie crust, better than Crisco I think.

Ste.Claire: Now could you just cut the fatback off the pig while he's still alive and he's running around? (laughing)

Gloria Burnell: Not hardly.

Dave Burnell: (tells pig joke)

Ste.Claire: Now what was the quickest and cheapest way of making coffee? ... I mean if you didn't have a percolator.

Gloria Burnell: You went to the store and you bought your own coffee beans and you grind them in a little coffee grinder.

Ste.Claire: OK.

Gloria Burnell: They sell coffee beans like in a round barrel like they used to do.

Ste.Claire: So you would bring home your coffee beans, and grind them up. Then you would have grounds and no coffee pot or maker ... what would you do, would you tie them up in something?

Dave Burnell: No. Put it right in the pot and put water in here and boil it.

Ste.Claire: OK, and then how would you separate the grounds?

Dave Burnell: Let it set.....let it set till it quit boiling and they'd go to the bottom.

Gloria Burnell: Till you got to the very last cup and then you'd have to be real careful or you got a lot of coffee grounds in with your cup of coffee...

Dave Burnell: Hell, my brother, I don't know whether he still does but he made his like that all the time.

Gloria Burnell: Yes, he didn't like the perked coffee or through the machines and all. Your coffee beans of course would of been imported in here from wherever they grew the coffee. Like Brazil or other countries. I don't know, if ever, of coffee being grown in this country though.

Dave Burnell: Well that guy out there he says rice was grew in Arkansas in.......

Gloria Burnell: Well where did we go through when we traveled and saw the rice fields?

Dave Burnell: Well Mississippi, Arkansas.....

Ste.Claire: What else did Crackers eat?

Dave Burnell: Mullet.

Ste.Claire: Did they eat mullet from around here, like in our local river.

Gloria Burnell: From the little streams off the rivers too.

Dave Burnell: I don't think you'd get too many back up there for the water gets fresh water....

Ste.Claire: Well, you know they'll swim up into fresh water.

Dave Burnell: Yeah they will.

Ste.Claire: I lived up on Blue Run (Rainbow River) ... that's what it was called for a long time. There's plenty of mullet up in the run. The locals call them chicken fish.

Dave Burnell: An oldtimer once said that's one reason why he'd never be in Florida without a cast net and an ax, for he'd eat swamp cabbage and mullet.

Ste.Claire: Have you ever made swamp cabbage?

Dave Burnell: We never had it much.

Gloria Burnell: We cut one and chopped it up and put cold peas with it and salad dressing.

Dave Burnell: I never did care for it much myself.

Gloria Burnell: To me it tasted like that heart that's in a cabbage. It tasted just like that.

Ste.Claire: That's exactly what it is, heart of palm.

Gloria Burnell: I made it just once or twice.

Suggested Reading

Marjorie Kinnan Rawlings, *Cross Creek Cookery*. New York: Charles Scribner's Sons, 1942.

Ernest Matthew Mickler, *White Trash Cooking*, 1986.

Notes

1. Marjorie Kinnan Rawlings, *Cross Creek*, 1942, pp. 208 - 209.

2. Ibid. p. 240.

3. Ibid. p. 67.

Jake Summerlin, "King of the Crackers," c. 1860s. Cattle barons like Summerlin were dominant figures of west Florida's cattle industry. He owned vast herds which roamed what is now Orange and Osceola Counties. Summerlin made most of his fortune selling his cattle to Spanish buyers from Cuba for gold. This photograph is a daguerreotype which required long exposure time and still sittings up to three minutes. The chair in photo is typical of those found in studios in the mid-19th century, indicating that Summerlin posed for this shot, possibly as a joke. Some of Summerlin's descendants claim that this "Crackerfied" version of the Cattle King hardly represents the real Jake. Photograph, Florida State Archives.

Florida Cracker Cowhunters

"(They) can conceive of no greater happiness to a dying mortal than to take the last expiring breath, holding a cow-whip in one hand and a cow's tail in the other."

— A CORRESPONDENT WRITING FROM PINE LEVEL, FLORIDA ABOUT CRACKER CATTLEFOLK IN THE LATE 1870s.

When Spanish explorer Juan Ponce de Leon sailed from Santo Domingo to St. Augustine in 1521, he carried with him six heifers and a single bull. From this original and modest stock, a vast Florida cattle population descended which today numbers in the millions.[1] Cattle ranching has since held its place in Florida history, shaping the rural cultural landscape of the territory for over four and half centuries. But it was during the second quarter of the 1800s, especially after the Armed Occupation Act of 1842, when raising cattle as a way

Florida Cracker Cowhunters, Green Cove Springs c. 1880. With their wool hats and general unkempt appearance, Florida Cracker cowhunters hardly resembled the noble cowboys of the Wild West made famous by artist Frederic Remington and others. Whip always in hand, the cowmen were ready to herd an errant cow or kill a rattlesnake with a single crack. Photograph, Florida State Archives.

> *"The men who took these jobs were lean and rough as a cob. They'd round up what the Crackers called scrub cattle and mass up here or over near Altoona and drive those lowing critters all the way to the packing house in Green Cove Springs. A typical drive would last about eight days. The cowboys let the cattle graze along the way so they wouldn't lose too much weight during the drive. (It was) 'a hard scrabble life.'"*

— JOURNALIST JOHN CARTER ON SEVILLE STOCKMAN CLAUDE YELVINGTON AND OTHER EARLY 20TH CENTURY "CUSSEDLY INDEPENDENT" COWHUNTERS.

of life became attractive and widespread. With the surging industry, a unique breed of Cracker cattlemen called cowhunters emerged.

The life of these early cowmen was lonely and hard, but well suited to the rugged existence Crackers already knew well. Cattle drives lasting months meant rounding up herds in remote marshes and dense scrub forests, encounters with snakes and wolves, stampedes, torrential thunderstorms, searing heat, and swarms of mosquitos. The evenings were spent around a campfire, drinking black coffee and telling stories, if they weren't too tired. Throughout the night the crashing sounds of cattle trampling down palmetto patches would be heard.

Many Crackers were attracted to the Cowhunter lifestyle. Work as a ranch hand was easily found back when cattle ranged free of fences across endless miles of Florida swamps, palmetto prairies and scrub forests. The Cracker cattle they drove were direct descendants of Andalusian cattle introduced to Florida by the Spanish and of British Colonial breeds from the upper South. This hardy Florida stock, gaunt and mean, was bred to withstand tropical heat, insect bites, and sparse native forage. Their ponies, too, had bloodlines going back to the Andalusian breeds of the Spanish conquistadors.

> *"We had but happened upon a band of cow-hunters returning homeward with their spoils, and the fightings of their imprisoned cattle were only less frightful than their own wild orgies."*

— LOUISE SEYMOUR HOUGHTON'S *EKONIAH SCRUB: AMONG FLORIDA LAKES*, 1880.

Called marshtackies, these small horses were favored by cowmen for their smooth ride, durability and quick maneuverability, and were well adapted to the Florida wilderness.[2]

A catchdog sleeps between cattle runs. From Florida Fancies *by F. R. Swift, 1903, p. 28.*

The cowmen seldom used a rope, as lariats were practically useless in the thick scrub. Instead they used catchdogs which were trained to cut out and literally "catch" an errant cow and hold its ear or nose in its teeth until a cowman arrived.

"These dogs, like most other 'deer dogs' in Florida were mongrels, a mixture of cur and hound, and trained to follow a warm trail very slowly"

— JAMES A. HENSHALL, M. D., CAMPING AND CRUISING IN FLORIDA, 1884.

They used twelve to eighteen foot rawhide and buckskin whips called drags to drive their cattle. The whip's loud, rifle-shot popping, audible for miles, moved cattle in a desired direction, with the whip rarely touching the cow. Cracker cowmen were expert bullwhippers who could kill snakes or stop a herd of stampeding cattle with a pop from their drag. The stockmen sometimes used whip-cracking codes to communicate messages to each other across the lonely range. Florida cattleman and historian Doyle Connor, Jr. explains that early cowhunter whips were made

"Never will forget one big stampede ... At Fort Basinger. Eleven hundred steers went into a stampede. We men heard it in time and run in every direction. The stampede headed for a big swamp. Wasn't a thing we could do. The next morning we followed the trail down to the edge of the swamp. We knowed that the ground was too soft for 'em to get across. They didn't, you couldn't see no cows at all. All you could see was horns, just a whole lake of horns."

— EARLY 1900s BLACK COWMAN LAWRENCE SILAS OF OSCEOLA COUNTY.

Wild Cracker Bull

Captain Francis Asbury Hendry, an early Florida pioneer and Cracker cattle king, drove herds through the Ft. Meade area in 1870. He later acquired 30,000 acres in Hendry county which eventually was named for him. The Captain's story of an encounter with an old vicious "cradle-headed" bull named Old Frostysides still is a legend among cowmen and illustrates the dangerous lives of Cracker cowhunters:

"Just as I was a-turnin the p'int of the bayhead, Old Frosty come out

of that swamp like a tornado, with a great load of vines around his horns. I spurred Jack and squared myself before him. Then I give him a few right smart cracks with my drag, tryin to turn him into the herd, but he kept comin for me full tilt. Back of me was a p'int of sawgrass, and there wasn't no way to run 'cept into that bog." After getting thrown from his mount into the bog, Hendry remembers "the first thing I seen when I raised up out of the mud was Old Frosty's eyes lookin green at me, his tongue out, with ropes of slobber streamin from his mouth and nostrils. He was all set to run me through ... how I did it, I don't know, but I snatched my hat off and swung it at him. The p'int of one horn stuck right through the crown, and rested square over Old Frosty's eyes so he couldn't see a thing. I guess it's still there yet, and I hope it'll rot there."

McClellan saddle, c. 1904. From the collection of The Museum of Arts and Sciences; gift of Phillip and Rita Curzio, Samsula, Florida. Once U.S. Army surplus easily afforded by cowhunters, vintage McClellan saddles have increased in value and are sought after today because of their comfort to both rider and horse. Photograph by Roger Simms, 1997.

from tanned buckskin, and many of these were fabricated by Seminole Indians. After the 1930s, the drags were made with cow hide. Original 19th century buckskin whips are hard to come by and are treasured by those cowmen who are fortunate to own one.

Aside from a good whip, the cowhunters carried few other things. Saddles were leftover Army-issue McClellans that had no saddle horn. Coffee was cooked in tin cans and firearms were mostly shotguns and pistols powerful enough to stop bears, mad Cracker bulls, and rustlers in their tracks. A leather "wallet" stored

"It didn't take much to get a bunch of cows jumping. A bear, a clap of thunder or about anything might cause 'em to break lose. I've been run over, stomped and throwed, but I've never had a bone broken."

— COWMAN AB WRIGHT ON STAMPEDING FLORIDA SCRUB CATTLE THAT WERE UNPREDICTABLE AND "WILDER THAN BUFFALO." FROM JOE AKERMAN'S FLORIDA COWMAN, A HISTORY OF FLORIDA CATTLE RAISING, 1976, P. 179.

clothes, if a change of clothing was needed. Very often the only extra clothes carried along would be a pair of pants with a hole cut into the crotch so that they could be carried on the saddle. To economize space, cowmen would sometimes store horse feed in the horned pants.[3] In the early days, each Florida range-rider carried a distinctive hand-forged iron brand to mark his cattle. When the brands on a cow's flank became hard to see in the thick Florida scrub, cowhunters cut notches in their stock's ear to identify them.

Cowmen slept through the night on the sandy ground, sometimes in heavy rainstorms, with little more than an old blanket to keep him warm. Food rations on the range were typically grits, hot biscuits, black coffee, and occasionally fresh meat, usually game. At times, a fat steer was killed at the beginning of a long drive to feed a camp. [4]

In many ways, the Florida range with its surly cowhunters, whip-popping cattle drives, feuds between ranches, and shoot-outs in the scrub was wilder than the West.

An early cowman's meal on the range might consist of a frying pan full of bacon into which canned tomatoes were added, a pot of grits, baked sweet potatoes and buttermilk biscuits from the saddlebag, topped off by some very strong coffee. Huge batches of cornbread, biscuits and syrup cookies

A cowhunter campfire. From Florida Fancies by F. R. Swift, 1903, p. 56.

Cracker cowhunters carried few possessions out on the range. Aside from a good whip, a cowman packed a blanket, cooking and eating utensils, and sometimes a change of clothes. Firearms were necessary, too, and these were usually shotguns forceful enough to stop man and beast. Army-issue McClellan saddles, leftovers from the Civil War, were preferred by cowhunters because they were cheap, provided good seat ventilation, and had no horns. Saddle horns were practically useless as cowhunters used whips and catch dogs to manage their cattle, not ropes which would have been tied off at the horn. Lariats and saddles with horns were used after the screw fly was introduced to Florida from Texas earlier this century, when individual treatment of cattle by the range riders required ropes. Photograph by Roger Simms, 1997.

were usually baked up by the womenfolk to be taken out to the cowhands. On extended cattle drives the meat and sausage were fried and then packed into 5 gallon tins and then fat poured over it in order for the meat to keep. Being cattle country a lot of beef was eaten. Many times in order for it to keep well it was smoked, which also helped to

"*Having established himself on a land of his own (presumedly by squatting), or a patch of Uncle Sam's, he, if he pleases, may become a grazier at small expense of labour or money. Having bought, borrowed or stolen a few head of cattle, he simply marks them and turns them out into the woods. In the spring he collects the calves and puts his brand on them ... catching them when a purchaser appears. In this way some of these Florida squatters accumulated vast herd of cattle without any exertion on their part. Nay, so careless of comfort are they that I am sure there are a few men in these forests owning 5,000 to 6,000 head of cattle who have not even milk for their coffee.*"

— JAMES STERLING, VISITING NORTH FLORIDA IN THE 1850s, EXPLAINS HOW CRACKER SETTLERS AMASSED CATTLE SO QUICKLY. FROM JOE AKERMAN'S *FLORIDA COWMAN, A HISTORY OF FLORIDA CATTLE RAISING*, 1976, P. 58.

tenderize it. This was a definite bonus when eating some of the early "scrub cows" which were known to be a tough and stringy meal. A young recruit temporarily stationed in Florida before being shipped off to the Spanish American War wrote home to tell his mother not to worry about him getting shot because he figured he was fairly well bullet-proof after eating a lot of our local "scrub-cow" beef.

Bone Mizell was the subject of a Frederic Remington painting entitled "A Cracker Cowboy," originally published in the August 1895 issue of Harper's New Monthly Magazine. *From a lithograph produced by Jim Bob Tinsley.*

Bone Mizell: Cowhunter Legend

If Florida cattle barons were Cowhunter Kings, then Cracker wag Bone Mizell was nothing less than a Crown Prince of all Cowmen, an heir-apparent, but never a king - not because he lacked the opportunity or the popular vote, but simply because he chose not to be "powerful" rich, at least not for more than a few days at a time. Morgan Bonaparte Mizell, known to his fellow cowmen and the law as just Bone, was a true legend in his own day, held in high esteem by his cowhunter peers for his free-spirited, hard-drinking, fun-loving approach to living. He was said to "outrope, outride, outshoot, and outdrink" any cowman in Florida. It is thought that the folk hero offered his unpredictable antics to all as some distraction from their hard lives as range riders.[5]

Morgan Bonaparte Mizell (1863 - 1921) was known simply as "Bone" to his friends and fellow cowhunters. Photograph, Florida State Archives; loan from Jim Bob and Dottie Tinsley.

It could be argued that Bone was the most famous of all Florida Cracker cowmen, as his reputation and storied life were heard around cowhunter campfires from one end of the state to the other. Frederic Remington, the famous 19th century artist had something to do with this, immortalizing Mizell in a painting called, "A Cracker Cowboy." Bone, on his mount and his dog at side, was sketched by Remington when he came to Arcadia in 1895 to illustrate and write about the Florida frontier. Folklore suggests that Remington sought out the well-known and free-living Mizell as his model of a Florida cowman, and paid him with drink.

While tales about Bone Mizell have been exaggerated over the years, his real life was colorful and represents well the eccentric lifestyle of a Cracker cowboy. He rustled cattle, branded his livestock with his teeth (by notching the cow's ears), and rode horses into bars and ordered drinks from the saddle. Once, he hitched a big-top tent to a passing freight train when a traveling circus banned him for attracting too much attention.

Known for his wild spending sprees and spur-of-the-moment generosity, Mizell was hardly driven by money and did not eagerly aspire to be wealthy. Mizell once took all of the money he made from the sale of his cattle and chartered a steamer to carry him and his friends up and down the St. Johns River. Mizell explained later to reporters that he was content with being "powerful rich" for one day, but was happy to return to his cowhunting existence.

"In the fall of 1896, Bone helped a friend out of a legal skirmish similar to one of his own. The friend was arrested for butchering a cow of questionable ownership. Although he was well known in DeSoto County as an upstanding citizen, he was worried about his upcoming trial. Bone made him an offer: 'You buy me a John B. Stetson hat, and I'll get you out of this in two minutes,' he said. 'How?' asked the friend. 'Just have them call me as a witness,' Bone answered. The cowboy agreed.

At the trial, various witnesses were questioned about earmarks, brands, time of day, and other facts concerning the case. Bone was put on the stand and testified that he had seen the alleged butchering. When asked where he was at the time, he replied, 'Bee Branch.' 'Where's Bee Branch?' queried the prosecutor. 'Everybody knows where Bee Branch is,' answered Bone. 'It's two or three hundred yards over in the next county.' The defense called for a dismissal on the grounds that the defendant could not be tried in Arcadia for an offense committed in an adjoining county. The case was thrown out of court, and Bone got his new Stetson."

— JIM BOB TINSLEY, *FLORIDA COW HUNTER: THE LIFE AND TIMES OF BONE MIZELL*, 1990.

At other times, he could be found riding through town rip-roaring drunk with dollar bills pinned to his pants and shirt. He was known to kindle his pipe with paper money, too.[6]

Bone Mizell's cow country antics were legendary. One day a judge fined Bone twenty dollars for wearing a hat into his courtroom. Mizell calmly counted out twenty dollars and twenty more and placed the money on the judge's bench. "You better take forty, suh, 'cause I walked in heah with my hat on, and I'm gonna walk out the same way." Another time Bone attended a camp revival meeting after a night out on the town. Hungover, hot and thirsty, Bone set his sights on a big pitcher of water on the pulpit. Bone was the first to volunteer when the preacher called for sinners to be prayed for at the altar.

While the preacher and congregation closed their eyes in prayer, Bone turned the pitcher up and gulped down all of the water.

"Them that's got, has got to lose. Them that hasn't, kaint."

— BONE MIZELL'S SIMPLE PHILOSOPHY OF LIFE.

Bone Mizell's hard-living lifestyle took its toll and on July 14, 1921 at the age of 58 he died under the influence in a railroad depot at Fort Ogden, Florida. Mizell and other legendary Cracker cowhunters will forever be etched in Florida folklore as enduring symbols of a time gone by, Old Florida, and the way things used to be on the Florida range.

SUGGESTED READING

Joe A. Akerman, Jr., *Florida Cowman, A History of Florida Cattle Raising.* Kissimmee, 1976.

George H. Dacy, *Four Centuries of Florida Ranching.* St. Louis, 1940.

Jim Bob Tinsley, *Florida Cow Hunter: The Life and Times of Bone Mizell.* Orlando: University of Central Florida Press, 1990.

NOTES

1. Janos Shoemyen, "Home on the Range," in *Born of the Sun*, 1975, p. 132.

2. Joe A. Akerman, Jr., *Florida Cowman, A History of Florida Cattle Raising.* Kissimmee, 1976; Charles W. Arnade, "Cattle Raising in Spanish Florida, 1513 - 1763." *Agricultural History* 35 (No. 3), 1961. Reprinted by the St. Augustine Historical Society, Publication No. 21, 1965; George H. Dacy, *Four Centuries of Florida Ranching.* St. Louis, 1940.

3. Interview with Doyle (D.J.) Connor, Jr., Florida cattle historian, December, 1996.

4. George H. Dacy, *Four Centuries of Florida Ranching.* St. Louis, 1940.

5. Jim Bob Tinsley, *Florida Cow Hunter: The Life and Times of Bone Mizell.* Orlando: University of Central Florida Press, 1990.

6. Ibid.

Frederic Remington in front of the fireplace at his New Rochelle, New York studio, c. late 19th century. Courtesy of the Frederic Remington Art Museum, Ogdensburg, N.Y.

Rogue Paradise:
Frederic Remington in Florida

"Two very emaciated Texas ponies pattered down the street, bearing wild-looking individuals, whose hair and drooping hats and generally bedraggled appearance would remind you at once of the Spanish-moss which hangs so quietly and helplessly to the limbs of the oaks out in the swamps ... So this is the Cracker cowboy, whose chief interest would be found in the tales of some bushwhacking enterprise, which I very much fear would be a one-sided story, and not worth the telling."

— FREDERIC REMINGTON, *CRACKER COWBOYS OF FLORIDA*, 1895.

While Cracker Florida has been romanticized over the past century in novels and folklore, not every early Florida visitor was fond of it. Perhaps its harshest critic was Frederic Sackrider Remington, famed 19th century artist and illustrator of frontier life, who came to south-central Florida seeking a bit of the Old West in the South. In an 1895 article in *Harper's New Monthly Magazine*, he painted a less than flattering portrait of the Cracker cowhunter and his surroundings in Arcadia, making it very clear that Florida was no the place for the respectable and more traditional cowboy to be. Hopelessly jaded by the West, Remington offered up the "barren" Florida landscape as "flat and sandy, with miles of straight pine timber, each tree an exact duplicate of its neighbor, and underneath the scrub palmettos, the twisted brakes and hammocks, and the gnarled water-oaks festooned with the sad gray Spanish-moss - truly not a country for a high spirited race or moral giants."

Remington, who spent a great deal of his life coloring the cowboy frontier in the West, made it no secret that he despised the Florida backwoods and Cracker lifestyle. He described the Cracker cowhunters as renegades who knew nothing about using a lariat, and was amazed at the fighting over such poor-grade cattle - "out in the wilderness low-browed cow-folks shoot and stab each other for the possession of scrawny creatures not fit for a pointer-dog to mess on." Despite his steadfast bias, Remington may have been partly right about the cattlehands, and surely their livestock and horses were nothing to brag about. Many Florida cowmen of Remington's day were drifting veterans of the Civil

"Fighting Over a Stolen Herd." Painting by Frederic Remington originally published in the August 1895 issue of Harper's New Monthly Magazine. *From a lithograph produced by Jim Bob Tinsley.*

War or fugitives seeking sanctuary. Some even amassed their herds by stealing cattle from each other - "they steal by wholesale, any cattle-hunter will admit; and why they brand at all I cannot see."

The artist and writer was also disillusioned by the immoral law of the land - "It is rarely that their affairs are brought to court, but when they are, the men come en masse to the room, armed with knives and rifles, so that any decision is bound to be a compromise, or it will bring on a general engagement."

Remington's accounts of Cracker cowboys and their reputations as ornery independents are not too far from the truth, but hardly the whole story. Remington, rarely spoke to ranchers and cattlehands, but instead interviewed bankers and store-keepers who did not care for the rogues.[1] The absence of roping techniques was also misinterpreted by Remington - lariats were all but useless in the thick scrub forests where riding horseback was difficult enough. Dogs were more useful to cattlehands for herding livestock and driving out cattle from the thick underbrush.

In one dark corner of his sweeping critique, Remington managed to find character, albeit faint, in the Cracker cowhunter way - "They are well paid for their desperate work, and always eat fresh beef or 'razor-backs' and deer which they kill in the woods. The heat, the poor grass, their brutality, and the pest of the flies kill their ponies, and as a rule, they lack dash and are indifferent riders, but they are picturesque in their unkempt, almost unearthly wildness." Remington's 1895 foray into Florida's "Wild West" was his first trip there, and his last.

Suggested Reading

Julian M. Pleasants, "Frederic Remington in Florida." *Florida Historical Quarterly* 61, no. 1 (July 1977): 1-12.

Notes

1.   Mark Derr, *Some Kind of Paradise: A Chronicle of Man and the Land in Florida.* New York: William Morrow and Company, 1989.

Cracker Cowboys of Florida

by Frederic Remington

Reproduced from the original *Harper's New Monthly Magazine* article, August, 1895.

One can thresh the straw of history until he is well worn out, and also is running some risk of wearing others out who may have to listen, so I will waive the telling of who the first cowboy was, even if I knew; but the last one who has come under my observation lives down in Florida, and the way it happened was this: I was sitting in a "sto' do'," as the "Crackers" say, waiting for the clerk to load some "number eights," when my friend said, "Look at the cowboys!" This immediately caught my interest. With me cowboys are what gems and porcelains are to some others. Two very emaciated Texas ponies pattered down the street, bearing wild-looking individuals, whose hanging hair and drooping hats and generally bedraggled appearance would remind you at once of the Spanish-moss which hangs so quietly and helplessly to the limbs of the oaks out in the swamps. There was none of the bilious fierceness and rearing plunge which I had associated with my friends out West, but as a fox terrier is to a yellow cur, so were these last. They had on about four dollars' worth of clothes between them and rode McClellan saddles, with saddle-bags, and guns tied on before. The only things they did which were conventional were to tie their ponies up by the head in brutal disregard, and then get drunk in about fifteen minutes. I could see that in this case, while some of the tail feathers were the same, they would easily classify as new birds.

"And so you have cowboys down here?" I said to the man who ran the meat-market.

He picked a tiny piece of raw liver out of the meshes of his long black beard, tilted his big black hat, shoved his arms into his white apron front, and said, "Gawd! yes, stranger; I was one myself."

The plot thickened so fast that I was losing much, so I became more deliberate. "Do the boys come into town often?" I inquired further.

"Oh yes, 'mos' every little spell," replied the butcher, as he reached behind his weighing-scales and picked up a double-barreled shot-gun,

"Cracker Cowboys of Florida." Painting by Frederic Remington originally published in the August 1895 issue of Harper's New Monthly Magazine. *From a lithograph produced by Jim Bob Tinsley.*

sawed off. "We-uns are expectin' of they-uns to-day." And he broke the barrels and took out the shells to examine them.

"Do they come shooting?" I interposed.

He shut the gun with a snap. "We split even, stranger."

Seeing that the butcher was a fragile piece of bric-a-brac, and that I might need him for future study, I bethought me of the banker down the street. Bankers are bound to be broad-gauged, intelligent, and conservative, so I would go to him and get at the ancient history of this neck of the woods. I introduced myself, and was invited behind the counter. The look of things reminded me of one of those great green terraces which conceal fortifications and ugly cannon. It was boards and wire screen in front, but behind it were shot-guns and six-shooters, hung in the handiest way, on a sort of disappearing gun-carriage arrangement. Shortly one of the cowboys of the street scene floundered in. He was two-thirds drunk, with brutal shifty eyes and a flabby lower lip.

"I want twenty dollars on the old man. Ken I have it?"

I rather expected that the bank would go into "action front," but the clerk said, "Certainly," and completed this rather odd financial transaction, whereat the bull-hunter stumbled out.

"Who is the old man in this case?" I ventured.

"Oh, it's his boss, old Colonel Zuigg, of Crow City. I gave some money to some of his boys some weeks ago, and when the colonel was down here I asked him if he wanted the boys to draw against him in that way, and he said, 'Yes—for a small amount; they will steal a cow or two, and pay me that way.' "

Here was something tangible.

"In Wait For An Enemy." Painting by Frederic Remington originally published in the August 1895 issue of Harper's New Monthly Magazine. *From a lithograph produced by Jim Bob Tinsley.*

"What happens when a man steals another man's brand in this country?"

"He mustn't get caught; that's all. They all do it, but they never bring their troubles into court. They just shoot it out there in the brush. The last time old Colonel Zuigg brought Zorn Zuidden in here and had him indicted for stealing cattle, said Zorn: 'Now see here, old man Zuigg, what do you want for to go and git me arrested fer? I have stole thousands of cattle and put your mark and brand on 'em, and jes because I have stole a couple of hundred from you, you go and have me indicted. You jes better go and get that whole deal nol prossed;' and it was done."

The argument was perfect.

"From that I should imagine that the cow-people have no more idea of law than the 'gray apes,' " I commented.

"Yes, that's about it. Old Colonel Zuigg was a judge fer a spell, till some feller filled him with buckshot, and he had to resign; and I remember he decided a case against me once. I was hot about it, and the old colonel he saw I was. Says he, 'Now yer mad, ain't you?' And I allowed I was. 'Well,' says he, 'you hain't got no call to get mad. I have decided the last eight cases in yer favor, and you kain't have it go yer way all the time; it wouldn't look right;' and I had to be satisfied."

The courts in that locality were but the faint and sickly flame of a taper offered at the shrine of a justice which was traditional only, it seemed. Moral forces having ceased to operate, the large owners began to brand everything in sight, never realizing that they were sowing the wind. This action naturally demoralized the cowboys, who shortly began to brand a little on their own account—and then the deluge. The rights of property having been destroyed, the large owners put strong outfits in the field, composed of desperate men armed to the teeth, and what happens in the lonely pine woods no one knows but the desperadoes themselves, albeit some of them never come back to the little fringe of settlements.

The winter visitor from the North kicks up the jack-snipe along the beach or tarponizes in the estuaries of the Gulf, and when he comes to the hotel for dinner he eats Chicago dressed beef, but out in the wilderness low-browed cow-folks shoot and stab each other for the possession of scrawny creatures not fit for a pointer-dog to mess on. One cannot but feel the force of Buckle's law of "the physical aspects of nature" in this sad country. Flat and sandy, with miles and miles of straight pine timber, each tree an exact duplicate of its neighbor tree, and underneath the scrub palmettoes, the twisted brakes and hammocks, and the gnarled water-oaks festooned with the sad gray Spanish-moss — truly not a country for a high-spirited race or moral giants.

The land gives only a tough wiregrass, and the poor little cattle, no bigger than a donkey, wander half starved and horribly emaciated in search of it. There used to be a trade with Cuba, but now that has gone; and beyond the supplying of Key West and the small fringe of settlements they have no market. How well the cowboys serve their masters I can only guess, since the big owners do not dare go into the woods, or even to their own doors at night, and they do not keep a light burning in the houses. One, indeed, attempted to assert his rights, but some one pumped sixteen buckshot into him as he bent over a spring to drink, and he left the country. They do tell of a late encounter between two rival foremen, who rode on each other in the woods, and drawing, fired, and both were found stretched dying under the palmettoes, one calling deliriously the name of his boss. The unknown reaches of the Everglades lie just below, and with a half-hour's start a man who knew the country would be safe from pursuit, even if it were attempted; and, as one man cheerfully confided in me, "a boat don't leave no trail, stranger."

That might makes right, and that they steal by wholesale, any cattle-hunter will admit; and why they brand at all I cannot see, since one boy tried to make it plain to me, as he shifted his body in drunken abandon and grabbed my pencil and a sheet of wrapping-paper: "See yer; ye see that?" And he drew a circle O and then another ring around it, thus: ◎. "That brand ain't no good. Well, then —" And again his knotted and dirty fingers essayed the brand | O. He laboriously drew upon it and made ⊖, which of course destroyed the former brand.

"Then here," he continued, as he drew **13**, "all ye've got ter do is this —**313**." I gasped in amazement, not at his cleverness as a brand-destroyer, but at his honest abandon. With a horrible operatic laugh, such as is painted in "the Cossack's Answer," he again laboriously drew ⊕, and then added some marks which made it look like this ⟟ And again breaking into his devil's "ha, ha!" said, "Make the damned thing whirl."

I did not protest. He would have shot me for that. But I did wish he was living in the northwest quarter of New Mexico, where Mr. Cooper and Dan could throw their eyes over the trail of his pony. Of course each man has adjusted himself to this lawless rustling, and only calculates that he can steal as much as his opponent. It is rarely that their affairs are brought to court, but when they are, the men come *en masse* to the room, armed with knives and rifles, so that any decision is bound to be a compromise, or it will bring on a general engagement.

There is also a noticeable absence of negroes among them, as they still retain some *ante bellum* theories, and it is only very lately that they have "reconstructed." Their general ignorance is "miraculous," and quite mystifying to an outside man. Some whom I met did not even know where the Texas was which furnishes them their ponies. The railroads of Florida have had their ups and downs with them in a petty way on account of the running over of their cattle by the trains; and then some long-haired old Cracker drops into the nearest station with his gun and pistol, and wants the telegraph operator to settle immediately on the

"A Bit of Cow Country." Painting by Frederic Remington originally published in the August 1895 issue of Harper's New Monthly Magazine. *From a lithograph produced by Jim Bob Tinsley.*

basis of the Cracker's claim for damages, which is always absurdly high. At first the railroads demurred, but the cowboys lined up in the "brush" on some dark night and pumped Winchesters into the train in a highly picturesque way. The trainmen at once recognized the force of the Crackers' views on cattle-killing, but it took some considerable "potting" at the more conservative superintendents before the latter could bestir themselves and invent a "cow-attorney," as the company adjuster is called, who now settles with the bushmen as best he can. Certainly no worse people ever lived since the big killing up Muscleshell way, and the romance is taken out of it by the cowardly assassination which is the practice. They are well paid for their desperate work, and always eat fresh beef or "razor-backs," and deer which they kill in the woods. The heat, the poor grass, their brutality, and the pest of the flies kill their ponies, and, as a rule, they lack dash and are indifferent riders, but they are picturesque in their unkept, almost unearthly wildness. A strange effect is added by their use of large, fierce cur-dogs, one of which accompanies each cattle-hunter, and is taught to pursue cattle, and even take them by the nose, which is another instance of their brutality. Still,

"Cowboys Wrestling a Bull." Painting by Frederic Remington originally published in the August 1895 issue of Harper's New Monthly Magazine. *From a lithograph produced by Jim Bob Tinsley.*

as they only have a couple of horses apiece, it saves them much extra running. These men do not use the rope, unless to noose a pony in a corral, but work their cattle in strong log corrals, which are made at about a day's march apart all through the woods. Indeed, ropes are hardly necessary, since the cattle are so small and thin that two men can successfully "wrestle" a three-year-old. A man goes into the corral, grabs a cow by one horn, and throwing his other arm over her back, waits until some other man takes her hind leg, whereat ensues some very entertaining Graeco-Roman style.

When the cow is successful, she finds her audience of Cracker cowboys sitting on the fence awaiting another opening, and gasping for breath. The best bull will not go over three hundred pounds, while I have seen a yearling at a hundred and fifty—if you, O knights of the riata, can imagine it! Still, it is desperate work. Some of the men are so reckless and active that they do not hesitate to encounter a wild bull in the open. The cattle are as wild as deer, they race off at scent; and when "rounded up" many will not drive, whereupon these are promptly shot. It frequently happens that when the herd is being driven quietly along a bull will turn on the drivers, charging at once. Then there is a scamper and great shooting. The bulls often become so maddened in these forays that they drop and die in their tracks, for which strange fact no one can account, but as a rule they are too scrawny and mean to make their handling difficult.

So this is the Cracker cowboy, whose chief interest would be found in the tales of some bushwacking enterprise, which I very much fear would be a one-sided story, and not worth the telling. At best they must be revolting, having no note of the savage encounters which used to characterize the easy days in West Texas and New Mexico, when every man tossed his life away to the crackle of his own revolver. The moon shows pale through the leafy canopy on their evening fires, and the mists, the miasma, and mosquitoes settle over their dreary camp talk. In place of the wild stampede, there is only the bellowing in the pens, and instead of the plains shaking under the dusty air as the bedizened vaqueros plough their fiery broncos through the milling herds, the cattle-hunter wends his lonely way through the ooze and rank grass, while the dreary pine trunks line up and shut the view.

Historic Cracker Sites of Florida

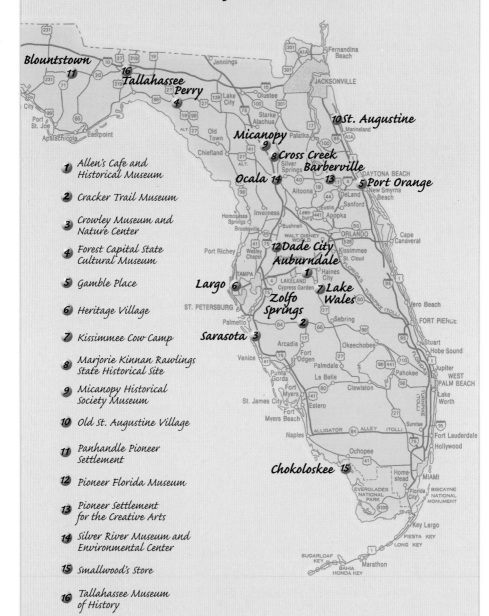

Blountstown 11
16 Tallahassee
Perry 4
Micanopy 9
8 Cross Creek
Ocala 14
Barberville
13
10 St. Augustine
5 Port Orange

12 Dade City
Auburndale
1
Largo 6
7 Lake Wales
Zolfo Springs
2
Sarasota 3
Chokoloskee 15

1 Allen's Cafe and Historical Museum

2 Cracker Trail Museum

3 Crowley Museum and Nature Center

4 Forest Capital State Cultural Museum

5 Gamble Place

6 Heritage Village

7 Kissimmee Cow Camp

8 Marjorie Kinnan Rawlings State Historical Site

9 Micanopy Historical Society Museum

10 Old St. Augustine Village

11 Panhandle Pioneer Settlement

12 Pioneer Florida Museum

13 Pioneer Settlement for the Creative Arts

14 Silver River Museum and Environmental Center

15 Smallwood's Store

16 Tallahassee Museum of History

Crackerdom: A Self-Guided Tour

The Geiger Residence, an "upscale" Cracker house in Micanopy, Florida. Photograph by Jean Hartline, 1997. (See page 206)

Crackerdom is rich and real in Florida with its rustic architecture, rural peoples and sprawling cattle ranches - you don't have to travel very far in the state to connect with Crackerfolk and their way of life. While immersing yourself in the Cracker lifestyle may be the surest route to understanding it, there are more accessible and less challenging ways of experiencing the culture. There are, for example, preserved or reconstructed Cracker houses at pioneer settlements and at museums across the state, most of which are available for interior touring, and many of which are filled with Cracker material culture. Occasionally, you will find an off-beat slice of Crackerdom like the Bone Mizell memorial plaque in Zolfo Springs or his grave in Arcadia.

Offered here is a sampling of Cracker venues throughout the state; it is by no means a complete inventory of Cracker sites in Florida. For those who want to fully explore Crackerdom in a particular area, the local Chamber of Commerce should be able to give you a full listing of Cracker sites and related special events like festivals and living history programs. Together, two or three of these stops will make for an enlightening day trip. Happy Cracker trails.

Allen's Cafe & Historical Museum

1837 Highway 92 Auburndale, Florida

Telephone: (941) 967-4307

With the closing of the Yearling Restaurant at Cross Creek, the number of eateries in Florida that serve authentic Cracker foods as a main course has become fewer and fewer. Perhaps the best of these is Allen's Cafe in Auburndale. The restaurant is famous for Cracker dishes like cooter, alligator, rattlesnake, armadillo, fried rabbit, quail and frog legs. And make sure you try Mrs. Jewell Allen's secret recipe of hand mixed hush-puppies. Allen's offers more traditional fare for the less adventurous.

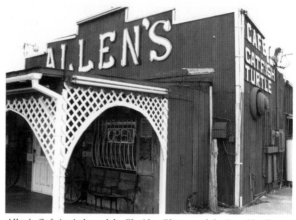

Allen's Cafe in Auburndale, Florida. Photograph by Jean Hartline, 1997.

An early Cracker cowhunter whip, one of many antiques visitors can find inside Allen's Cafe & Historical Museum. Photograph by Jean Hartline, 1997.

Founded by the late Carl Allen, author of *Root Hog or Die Poor*, and his wife Jewell, the Cafe has operated at the same Auburndale location for well over 35 years.

Inside is a fascinating collection of early American antiques and many Cracker items. Every Thursday evening there is a blue grass jam in the Big Pickin' Parlour. Pickers from all over the country come to pick on stage, in one of the three dining rooms, or out on the front porch.

Allen's Cafe is open every day except Monday. Reservations are required September - April for the Thursday Parlour Show with dinner. The restaurant is located on Route 92 between Winter Haven and Lakeland. Look for a red building with white lattice.

Cracker Trail Museum

HARDEE COUNTY PIONEER PARK

2822 MUSEUM DRIVE ❖ ZOLFO SPRINGS, FLORIDA

TELEPHONE: (941) 735-0119

Located on the historic Peace River and along the original Cracker Trail, Pioneer Park is home to the 1879 Hart log cabin and the 1886 "Cracker Trail" post office. The Museum interprets the history of Peace River pioneer people, among other things. But most important, make sure you ask the Cracker Trail folks for directions to the famous Bone Mizell Historic Monument at Zolfo Springs. Bone is just commemorated here, however. The celebrated Florida Cracker cowhunter is buried in Arcadia.

Pioneer Park is open Thur.-Mon., 9:00 a.m. - 6:00 p.m. It is located off U.S. 17 at Zolfo Springs.

The Bone Mizell Historic Monument in Zolfo Springs. Photograph courtesy John Tyson, 1997.

The Cracker Trail Post Office. Photograph courtesy John Tyson, 1997.

Crowley Museum
and Nature Center

16405 MYAKKA ROAD SARASOTA, FLORIDA

TELEPHONE: (941) 322-1000

The design, materials and methods of construction of the 1889 Tatum House are typical of late 19th century residences in rural Florida. Photograph c. 1950s, courtesy of the Crowley Museum and Nature Center.

Crowley Museum, located on a 185 acre wildlife sanctuary on the Myakka River, is home to a pioneer history center which interprets early Florida life. On site is the Tatum House, a two-story, circa 1889 "Cracker" house and one of the oldest examples of rural architecture in Sarasota County today. Nearby is the "Homesteader," a reconstructed one room "pioneer" cabin filled with furnishings and utensils from the late 19th century. Visitors can also walk a section of the original Pine Level Trail which connected the early Cracker settlements of Pine Level and Braidentown.

The Museum is open to for tours Friday, Saturday, and Sunday, 10:00 a.m. - 1:00 p.m.

Two hour guided tours are available. Schools and group tours available by appointment. Hours subject to change, call for confirmation. Admission is a suggested $5.00 donation for adults; children 12 and under enter free.

Forest Capital
State Cultural Museum

204 FOREST PARK DRIVE ⬛ PERRY, FLORIDA 32347

TELEPHONE: (904) 584-3227

For Cracker architecture enthusiasts, the Widdon log cabin at the Forest Capital Museum is a must-see. Constructed in 1864, the house was moved to its present location in 1972. The cabin has a dog-trot or breezeway which separates two single room cabins and wide porches. Wedge shaped piers keep the house off the damp ground.

While there are more popular examples of Cracker architecture, the Widdon House is perhaps the purist example of a surviving backwoods Cracker dog-trot dwelling in Florida. Ronald Haase features the rustic log cabin in his book, *Classic Cracker: Florida's Wood-Frame Vernacular Architecture* (Pineapple Press 1992, pages 34 - 42).

The Forest Capital State Cultural Museum is open Thursdays - Mondays 9:00 a.m. - 12 noon and 1:00 p.m. - 5:00 p.m.; it is closed Tuesdays and Wednesdays. Admission is $1.00; children under the age of six enter free. The Museum is located on U.S. 19-27 one mile south of Perry.

The 1864 Widdon log cabin at the Forest Capital Museum is one of the best examples of Cracker architecture in Florida. Photograph courtesy Forest Capital State Cultural Museum.

Gamble Place

FLORIDA HISTORY EDUCATION CENTER

THE MUSEUM OF ARTS AND SCIENCES ◈ PORT ORANGE, FLORIDA

TELEPHONE: (904) 255-0285

Gamble Place features the Cracker-style country retreat of Ivory Soap king James Gamble, a turn-of-the-century cottage on the banks of Spruce Creek in

western Port Orange. In 1907, Gamble incorporated many Florida "cracker" elements into a bungalow design, a reflection of his fondness for country architecture and lifestyle. The house features crescent moons on the shutters, a

Gamble Place, James Gamble's upscale version of a Cracker house. Photograph by Dana Ste.Claire, 1991.

well known southern motif found on many "outbuildings" throughout the rural South and, of historic note, half of the Procter and Gamble logo.

The rustic retreat is Gamble's upscaled interpretation of a Cracker house, but the unpretentious country

The spacious front porch of the Gamble House is filled with rustic cypress furniture. Photograph by Dana Ste.Claire, 1991.

flavor of the cottage is immediately recognizable with its wide veranda and breezeway. The home is of an unusual, yet magical, composition - clearly part hunting lodge, part fishing cabin, part "Thoreauish" retreat, and part Cracker country home, where front porches were frequented for chair-rocking socials well into the evening.

Gamble Place is open to the public Wednesdays and Saturdays and during special events. School group tours are available throughout the week. All visitation is by reservation through The Museum of Arts and Sciences (904) 255-0285. Directions to the Center, which includes the "Cracker" house, an early orange packing barn, the 1937 fantasy architecture Snow White House and a reconstructed Timucuan Indian village, are provided when reservations are made.

Heritage Village

PINELLAS COUNTY HISTORICAL MUSEUM

11909 125TH STREET NORTH LARGO, FLORIDA

TELEPHONE: (904) 584-3227

Heritage Village houses one of the largest collections of historical buildings in the state. Cracker buffs will want to see the McMullen-Coachman log home, the oldest structure in Pinellas County. Built in 1852, the dog-trot log cabin is typical of the houses mid-19th century Crackers built in region. The house features heart pine logs, ten-inch wide pine plank floors, a porch supported by cypress stumps, and a roof covered by hand-rived cypress shingles. The cabin's original chimney was made of mud and sticks, but later replaced by hand-made bricks. The house was moved to its present location from Clearwater in 1977.

The Village is open Tuesdays - Saturdays, 10 a.m. - 4 p.m. and Sundays 1 - 4 p.m.; it is closed on Mondays and during holidays. From September to May, afternoon visits are encouraged due to a busy morning schedule of school tours. Admission is free but donations are accepted.

McMullen Log House, c. 1852. Photograph courtesy Pinellas County Historical Museum.

Kissimmee Cow Camp

LAKE KISSIMMEE STATE PARK

14248 CAMP MACK ROAD ◈ LAKE WALES, FLORIDA

TELEPHONE: (941) 696-1112

The Kissimmee Cow Camp is a re-creation of a circa 1876 Cracker cowhunter camp complete with supply chuck wagon, horses, whips, saddles, and cooking utensils. Interpreted by State Park rangers, the camp allows visitors to experience firsthand what is was like to live and work cattle in 19th century Florida. More than 200 acres of land are used to maintain the park's herd of Cracker cattle, one of the few remaining herds of scrub cows in existence.

The living history site is open weekends and holidays from 9:30 a.m. to 4:30 p.m. Lake Kissimmee State Park is located 15 miles east of Lake Wales off Camp Mack Road.

Marjorie Kinnan Rawlings State Historical Site

STATE ROAD 325   CROSS CREEK, FLORIDA
TELEPHONE: (352) 466-9273

The Rawlings House is perhaps the most famous Cracker site in Florida. It was here that the famous Pulitzer Prize-winning author sat on her front porch and composed such classics as *The Yearling* and *Cross Creek*. Rawlings lived at the house alone through the Great Depression and into better times, garnering rich experiences from her Cracker neighbors for her works.

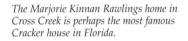

The Marjorie Kinnan Rawlings home in Cross Creek is perhaps the most famous Cracker house in Florida.

The house was assembled in the late 19th century and may contain all or parts of as many as three smaller houses joined together. During her stay, Rawlings added indoor plumbing, a carport, and screened the front porch. Most popular is the Cracker kitchen where many of Rawling's celebrated recipes were created and tested. Nearby visitors will find a reconstructed barn, a chicken coop, a well-manicured citrus grove and a country garden.

The Marjorie Rawlings' house is open to public tours Thursday through Sunday from 10 a.m. to 4 p.m., with tours starting on the hour except at noon. Admission is $2.00 for adults and $1.00 for children 6 - 12; children five and under are free. Each tour is limited to 10 people. A waiting time is not unusual especially during the afternoon when tours fill up quickly.

Cross Creek is located on State Road 325 about 20 miles southeast of Gainesville. It is easily accessible from Interstate 75, U.S. 441 or U.S. 301.

Marjorie Kinnan Rawlings State Historical Site. Photograph by Roger Simms, 1997.

Micanopy Historical Society Museum

CORNER CHOLOKKA BOULEVARD AND BAY STREET MICANOPY, FLORIDA

TELEPHONE: (352) 466-3200

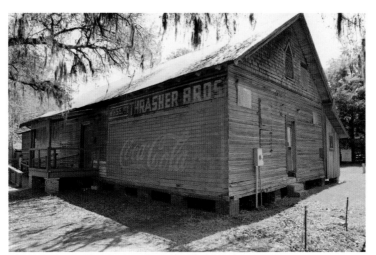

The 19th century Thrasher Warehouse, home of the Micanopy Historical Society Museum. Photograph by Roger Simms, 1997.

Micanopy has its own distinctive Cracker flavor and is a town worth exploring for its folksy architecture, old book shops and antique stores. A great place to start is at the Micanopy Historical Society Museum which is housed in the old Thrasher Warehouse. This frame building, famous for its early 20th century hand-painted Coca-Cola advertisement and the subject of many photographs, once served as a circa 1890s storehouse for a nearby general store. Among many things, the Museum features an interesting exhibit on the Micanopy-based Cracker cowhunter.

Down a side road is the Geiger Residence, an excellent example of a four-square Georgian Cracker house. The picture-perfect house is featured in Ronald Haase's *Classic Cracker: Florida's Wood-Frame Vernacular Architecture* (Pineapple Press 1992, pages 65 - 66).

The Museum is open Wednesdays and Fridays through Sundays from 1 - 4 p.m. Groups can be accommodated by appointment. The Geiger Residence is a private home but can be viewed during streetside touring. Self-guided tours of Micanopy are available at the Museum.

Micanopy is ten miles south of Gainesville off U.S. 441 and I-75. The Marjorie Kinnan Rawlings State Historical site is just down the road to the west. Together, the two sites make for a wonderful day trip.

Old St. Augustine Village

250 St. George Street ▧ St. Augustine, Florida

Telephone: (904) 823-9722

Old St. Augustine Village is a unique museum complex made up of nine historic houses and gardens dating back to the 1700s. Bounded by the narrow brick streets of St. George, Bridge and Cordova, the Village occupies an entire city block in St. Augustine's oldest historic district. When the museum opens in 1999, visitors will see the "Cracker Culture in Florida History" exhibition neatly housed in the 1899 Star General Store, a fully restored Cracker country market place.

The Cracker exhibit features an authentic covered wagon, an original mule cart, a moonshine still, photo murals of Cracker life, over 100 objects which relate to the Cracker culture, and as a signature piece, a Cracker store complete with a large cast-iron grits grinder, store-boughten' whiskey jugs, and other dry goods.

Village visitors will tour a series of fully-enclosed interrelated historic house museums, with each house featuring exhibitions and interpretation which address specific elements of Florida history. The 1790 Prince Murat House, 1830s Dow house, and seven other historic houses

Cracker store interior in the "Cracker Culture in Florida History" exhibition, Old St. Augustine Village, Museum of Arts and Sciences. Photograph by Roger Simms, 1997.

will be connected by a thematic and concurrent historical storyline with interpretive "bridges" between stops. The museum will offer a broad range of Florida history programs, including gallery tours, lectures, historic house tours, regular living history events, audiovisual presentations, computer interactive stations, and special workshops and courses for adults and children.

The Old St. Augustine Village, the city's "little Colonial Williamsburg," is located on St. George Street, two blocks south of the main Plaza, and catty-corner to the Lightner Museum.

Panhandle Pioneer Settlement

BLOUNTSTOWN, FLORIDA

TELEPHONE: (850) 674-8055

Silas Green and Ma Wood greet visitors from the front porch of the Yon Farm House at the Panhandle Pioneer Settlement. Photograph by Kathy Johnson, Calhoun County Record.

The Panhandle Pioneer Settlement has preserved a slice of turn-of-the-century rural Florida life for visitors to experience. Among the historic buildings at the Settlement is the Civil War period Bailey Log Home. Built around 1860, the round log house features deep front and back porches and roof-over-side steps. Additional rooms and porches were added to the cabin as its Cracker occupants could afford to. A stick and mud fireplace was replaced with brick, which was used for decades to prepare meals for the family.

The Panhandle Pioneer Settlement is open Saturdays from 2 - 4 p.m. and during scheduled special events. Admission is $1.00 for adults, 50 cents for children 6 - 18; children under six enter free.

The Bailey Log Home. Photograph by Ronnie Stone, 1996.

Pioneer Florida Museum

15602 PIONEER MUSEUM ROAD   ▣   DADE CITY, FLORIDA
TELEPHONE: (904) 567-0262

The Pioneer Florida Museum is a collection of seven buildings, five of which are historic structures, including the Civil War period John Overstreet House, a two-story farmhouse constructed of native heart pine. The pine was cut with a primitive, steam-run band saw and hand tools, and the floor joists were held together with wooden pegs.

The John Overstreet house, c. 1860s.

The Overstreet House is thought to be the oldest building from Pasco County. In the 19th century, the house lodged pioneers who would pay for their boarding either with money or produce. Pioneers traveling by wagon or on horseback would stay at the house overnight or longer while they cleared their land and built cabins.

The Pioneer center also features antique farm equipment, a barn with a branding iron collection, and original brand records of Pasco County cattle ranchers.

The Museum is open Tuesdays through Sundays from 1 - 5 p.m. and closed on Monday and on major holidays. There is usually a small admission charge.

The Pioneer Florida Museum is located one mile north of Dade City. From Dade City, take U.S. 301 north to Pioneer Museum Road.

Pioneer Settlement
for the Creative Arts

1776 LIGHTFOOT LANE BARBERVILLE, FLORIDA

TELEPHONE: (904) 749-2959

The Pioneer Settlement in Barberville is one of Florida's most unique and most active heritage and folk centers. On site are many historic buildings which

The Country Store c. 1884. Pioneer Settlement for the Creative Arts, Barberville. Photograph by Roger Simms, 1997.

have been moved to and preserved on the Settlement grounds, including an early railroad depot, a brick turpentine still, a bridgehouse, and a commissary store. Cracker buffs will want to stop by the Lewis Log Cabin, built in south Georgia around 1870 by Jim Lewis. In 1991, the Cracker cabin was purchased by Lewis' descendants and donated to the Settlement. It was dismantled and reconstructed on its present site in 1992.

The Settlement hosts special events and activities throughout the year, but the one not to miss is their fall Jamboree which attracts thousands of visitors from around the state. At the event, it is common to see Crackers grinding grits and cutting timbers the "old fashion" way.

Visiting hours are from 9 a.m. to 4 p.m. Mondays through Fridays, with the last tour starting at 3 p.m., and from 9 a.m. to 1 p.m. on Saturdays. The center is closed on Sundays and holidays. Admission is $2.50 for adults, $1.50 for children ages 5 - 18; those under five enter free.

The Pioneer Settlement is located just west of the intersection of U.S. 40 and Hwy. 17 in Barberville, about 20 miles west of Ormond Beach, 15 miles north of DeLand, and 50 miles east of Ocala.

The Lewis Log Cabin c. 1870 at Barberville. Photograph by Roger Simms, 1997.

Silver River Museum and Environmental Center

7189 N.E. 7TH STREET   OCALA, FLORIDA
TELEPHONE: (352) 236-5401

The Godwin Cracker House (top and bottom). Silver River Museum and Environmental Center, Ocala. Photographs by Roger Simms, 1997.

The Silver River Museum itself is worth seeing, but make sure you visit the Godwin family Cracker homestead site. Meticulously reconstructed, the homestead is a replica of a late 19th century Florida "Cracker" settlement complete with log home, barn, smokehouse, well, boiling shed, wash shed, potato bank, cane press, hog pen, mule pen, poultry pen and outhouse. There are many on-site opportunities for visitors to experience the Cracker way of life, including grits-grinding and sweeping with straw brooms.

The Museum is open every weekend from 9:00 a.m. - 5:00 p.m., and during special events. Public admission is $2.00. It is located south of the Silver Springs attraction on 7th Street.

Smallwood's Store

This one is way down there, but well worth seeing. Established by Ted Smallwood in 1906, Smallwood's Store and Ole Indian Trading Post is one of the few remaining original Cracker dry goods stores in Florida. For decades, it was the only trading post in this remote southwest Florida region where settlers

Heidi Cambata on the front porch of Ted Smallwood's Store and Ole Indian Trading Post, Chokoloskee. Photograph by Jean Hartline, 1993.

could get food and supplies. The old store is located on the western edge of the Everglades deep in the heart of the 10,000 Islands on Chokoloskee Island, one of Florida's last frontiers. Ted Smallwood traded with the Cracker settlers and Seminole Indians who lived throughout what is now known as the Everglades National Park, providing them with supplies such as coffee, sugar, flour, grits and cloth in exchange for hides, furs, venison, turtle, turkey, fish and other game. Remarkably, when the store was closed, 90% of the original goods remained in the store. Today, it is a wonderful time capsule for Florida Cracker history.

Smallwood's Store is open daily from December 1 - May 1, 10:00 a.m. - 5.00 p.m., and from May 2 - November 30 on Fridays - Tuesdays, 10:00 a.m. - 4:00 p.m.

Interior of Ted Smallwood's Store and Ole Indian Trading Post, Chokoloskee, Florida. Photograph by Jean Hartline, 1993.

Tallahassee Museum of History and Natural Science

3945 MUSEUM DRIVE   ▣   TALLAHASSEE, FLORIDA

TELEPHONE: (850) 575-8684

The Tallahassee Museum has re-created an extensive 1880 pioneer farmstead and community which includes the McNair-Black House, a Cracker-style hewn heart pine log farmhouse typical of those built by the earliest settlers of north Florida.

The form and construction of the log house could date as early as 1845, making it one of the earliest structures of its type in the state. It is featured in Ronald Haase's *Classic Cracker: Florida's Wood-Frame Vernacular Architecture* (Pineapple Press 1992, pages 29 - 31).

The Museum is open Mondays through Saturdays 9 a.m. - 5 p.m. and on Sundays 12:30 - 5 p.m. Admission is $6.00 for adults, $5.50 for seniors, and $4.00 for children.

The McNair-Black House c. 1845. Tallahassee Museum of History and Natural Science. Photograph courtesy of Linda Deaton, Tallahassee Museum.

A 19th century pipe-smoking cracker schoolmarm. From F.D. Srygley's Seventy Years in Dixie, *1891.*

Shud've Learnt That Befur:
Speaking the Cracker Tongue

The Florida Crackers have added their original and varied contribution to the lore and custom of the State including making their mark on the English language with their own southern dialect and unusual corruptions of words. Even today, Crackers speak a mixture of Old English provincialisms, local slang and a colorful array of home-spun words and crackerisms, like "as pleased as a blind hog findin' an acorn tree." The Florida Cracker vocabulary is as down-home and inventive as the people themselves.

Brushpoppers - Florida cowhunters. Called this as Teresa Stein explains in her *Florida Cracker Tales* (1995) because a rider, mounted on his marshtackie, went into the prairie brush and popped out one cow at a time.

catchdogs - Cracker cattle-herding dogs trained to literally "catch" a cow and hold its ear or nose in its teeth until a cowman arrived.

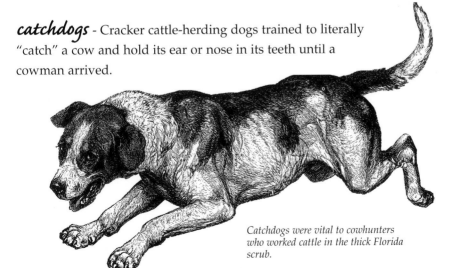

Catchdogs were vital to cowhunters who worked cattle in the thick Florida scrub.

217

chit'lins - Cracker version of chitterlings or hog innards, cleaned and cooked.

conchs - Crackers born in the Florida keys.

cooter - Freshwater turtles eaten by Crackers. Cracker purists will tell you that just the soft-shelled variety is a cooter, but others include the gopher tortoise, the hard-shell turtle, and the highly prized alligator snapping turtle.

corn pone - A "dressed-up" hoecake, made with the standard cornmeal, but milk instead of water was used in the batter. Corn pone differs from cornbread in that the former is fried and the latter is baked.

> *"If you would mention the word brassiere, a 'Cracker' would think you were speaking of some French fruit."*
>
> — CARL DANN, *VICISSITUDES AND CASATHROPHICS*, 1929.

Cracker - a self-reliant, independent and tenacious settler of the Deep South, often of Celtic stock, who subsisted by farming or raising livestock and, as a general rule, valued personal independence and restraint-free life over material prosperity. Cracker settlers provided a spirited foundation for the peopling of the rural South and Florida.

cracklin' - Crisp shreds of hog fat left over from making lard, sometimes mixed into meal to make cracklin' corn bread. In Harper Lee's *To Kill a Mockingbird*, Calpurnia shows her affection for the Finch family by baking them a pan of cracklin' cornbread.

A Florida curlew.

croaker sack - Burlap gunny sack sometimes used for clothing.

curlew - Pink spoon bills hunted for food and for their plumes.

drag - A rawhide whip used by Crackers for driving cattle or wagon oxen.

Freshwater turtles called "cooters" were a favorite Cracker staple. From The Great South *by Edward King, 1875, p. 535.*

fatback - Called fatback because this is exactly where it comes from - off the back of a hog. It was cut in small squares and put in cooking pots to flavor beans and other vegetables. Sometimes, it was roasted until it became crunchy and eaten like popcorn for a snack. Lard was made by boiling the fatback and straining it through fine cloth.

"A Southern Distillery." From Harper's New Monthly Magazine *1857, p. 733.*

fetch - To get, as in to "fetch" some water..

grits - A principal Cracker staple made from dried and coarsely ground corn, used in place of potatoes, never as a cereal. Hominy grits, not to be confused with hominy corn, is a Northern label for white grits.

hoecake - Primitive breadcake made of cornmeal, salt and water and cooked in an iron griddle or skillet. It is said that these cakes were once baked on a garden hoe held over an open fire.

holler - From the Appalachian foothills north it is a slope of land between two ridges; south of this, it means to shout.

hominy - Whole grains of corn soaked in lye-treated water for food.

"The cracker population have a drawling way of speaking and use a great many words like the backwoods population of North Carolina. It is a crackerism, not a specimen of the English language."

— FROM THE DIARY OF HENRY BENJAMIN WHIPPLE WHO
TOURED THE DEEP SOUTH FROM 1843 - 1844.

Knothead - A Cracker scrub cow.

literd - Fat pine or a hot fire started with fat pine. David Newell in his *If Nothin' Don't Happen* (1975) has this to say about the tender: "We get most of our kindlin' wood out in the flatwoods, just pickin' up light'd snags and knots. When lightnin' kills a pine tree, the sap wood rots off, leavin' the heart, which is full of turpentine and turns hard as iron ... The more turpentine gum there is in a light'd knot, the 'fatter' it is, and a feller can take a chunk of fat light'd and it'll catch afire almost like gasoline."

low bush lightning - Cracker term for moonshine, liquor made and smuggled during prohibition. The unusual names comes from the copper moonshine stills that were hidden away in the dense scrub bush and palmetto flatwoods.

marshtackie - A small horse with a narrow chest, prized by cowmen for their smooth ride, durability and quick maneuverability. Descendants of the horses brought to Florida by the Spanish, they are well adapted to the Florida wilderness.

pilau - Any dish of meat and rice cooked together, like a chicken pilau. Pronounced "per-loo" and spelled "perleu" by Crackers.

piney-woods rooter - Wild hog and a regular part of the Cracker diet. Known for their foul disposition, rooters regularly killed and ate rattlesnakes, and occasionally battled with alligators.

poultices - Medicinal salves made with materials such as soap, fat meat, chewing tobacco, chopped onion, scraped Irish potato, wet baking soda.

pull - To take a hard drink from a liquor jug.

rot gut - Bad whiskey.

sawmill chicken - Salt pork.

scrub chicken - Gopher tortoise, once a Cracker delicacy now illegal to take.

scrub cows - Cracker cattle bred to withstand the tough conditions of the Florida range. They are descendants of original Spanish cattle introduced to Florida in 1521.

swamp cabbage - The tender heart of Sabal Palm, cut and boiled like cabbage.

store-boughten - Crackers goods, sometimes beyond the means of Crackers, which could only be purchased from a store.

truck garden - A plot garden which was grown to produce a surplus of vegetables for sale to local grocery stores, etc.

varmit - The Cracker version of varmint, or any small animal, especially rodents.

whichaway - in which direction.

Takin' a "pull" from a whiskey jug. From Florida Fancies *by F. R. Swift, 1903, p. 58.*

Some Florida Crackerisms
and Cracker Philosophies . . .

I done drunk outa fruit jars so long I got a ridge acrosst my nose.

I just can't stand to wear shoes around home and I only put them on when I know company is comin or when I go to town. I wouldn't even put them on to go to town, but everybody else wears them and a person has to sorta dress like others do.

I don't wanta move to town; the rich are too crooked, and the poor are too mean.

I've got two dollars in my pocket, my wife don't eat much, my father gets a pension, and my mother's dead - so what've I got to worry about.

All the dog meat I have eaten in the name of sweet charity would stretch around the world.

If you burns your onion skins in the stove it'll keep quarrellin' outen the house.

— FROM A FT. MCCOY CRACKER,
IN MARJORIE KINNAN RAWLING'S SOUTH MOON UNDER.

I don't read papers much cause I feel that what the other feller is doin is no concern of mine.

I know I look older for I'm so thin and my hair is so gray but I've had a hard life and had so many children but I am not yet 50 but will be soon.

I ain't exactly a cracker, but I'm a southerner, and mighty proud of it, too.

My wife understands me and I understand her. If we don't agree I'll get me another woman.

I don't know what day it is, I'm just livin.

I reckon as how a change would do us both good, but we ain't got no place to change to.

Our main food is beans, grits, potatoes, cabbage, light bread and once in awhile some hamburger. It's the best I can do with $5 a week to spend on the table.

We are happy when we have some good eats and know where some more is comin from.

I needs lots of stuff but I got just anuff change for some beans and salt pork.

If any white varmits is so dumb or contrary as to come skulkin round my place, trespassin on private property, I'll blast em with hog shot and nail their pelts to the wall.

We have to take our bath in the tub I wash the clothes in.

I built a nice little house with wood floors - no more dirt floors, and a fireplace and windows, too.

Every time they scrub the floors upstairs it leaks through down here all over.

UNLESS NOTED, CRACKERISMS WERE COLLECTED FROM THE STETSON KENNEDY FILES, FLORIDA STATE ARCHIVES, TALLAHASSEE.

Cracker Prose

Over the years, some colorful prose has been penned by Crackers and firsthand observers of the Cracker culture. It is verse that is usually rich in tradition and often written with a good dose of humor, capturing well the spirit of Crackerness and the age-old art of front porch storytelling. Here are a few examples ...

I Want To Be A Florida Cracker

by Clifford J. Buckosh (1977)

Wish my mamma knew how to cook swamp cabbage
Wish my daddy had a rattlesnake hide
Wish I knew how to fix some conch fritters
Wish I had me a Seminole bride.

Chorus:
I want to be a Florida Cracker
But I'll never get a chance to try
I want to be a Florida Cracker
But I'll be a damn Yankee 'til I die.

Love them alligator, pink flamingo
Kumquat, avocado, Key Lime pie
Can't get enough of that
Sunshine surf's up
Never get enough of that clear blue sky.

Osceola, Flagler, Ponce', Menendez
All knew that they found something good
Key West smugglers, Tarpon sponge divers
Never would leave even if they could.

From *Cracker Cookin'* by B. J. Altschul, LaFray Publishing Co., 1984.

The Florida Cracker

by Pleasant Donald Gold

It's curious how things have changed in
thirty years or more,
There were no subdivisions then and every one was poor
If we sold a hundred acres, 'bout all we
got was thanks,
So in summer we skinned gators and in
Winter we skinned Yanks.
'Twas then we called folks crackers who
had lived here all the while
But now its so fine in Florida, it's gettin'
to be the style
To be called a Florida cracker if they
ain't been here a year,
And you'd think the guy who came last
week was a bloomin' pioneer.

But I can well remember when back in eighty-five,
(Then skeeters, snakes and 'gators were
as thick as bees in hive)
A cracker was a big white boss who gave
his lash a crack,
That sounded like a pistol shot across his
oxen's back.
And when from out the piney woods he'd
travel all the day,

To reach the nearest settlement, you could
hear some Yankee say:
"Here comes a Florida cracker to sell his
turpentine,"
For even then some Yankees knew the
value of the shine.
But now those good old days are gone and
the auto takes the place
Of the carry-log cart and the pair of
steers that moved with poky pace
Along the trail beneath the pines, knee
deep in grinding sand,
Where now the asphalt road leads on far
away across the land.
And where one time the bear and deer
roamed free o'er hill and dell,
Now stands the palace of the rich or a
spick and span hotel,
Or a golf course wide with eighteen holes,
where men and women play.
(We crackers watch their carryin's on and
wonder how they pay.)

From the Donald Bostrom Collection

The Ballad of Bone Mizell

by Ruby Leach Carson, c. 1930s
Music by Dottie & Jim Bob Tinsley

In Kissimmee they tell of old M. Bone Mizell
And the stranger who died on his hands;
How he died in dry season, and that was the reason
He was buried awhile on Bone's lands.

He was buried awhile on a palm and pine isle
In a swamp under Florida's sun
By the cowboy who nursed him, who loved him and cursed him
Just before his demise had begun.

"Jus' take the news ka'mly," Bone wrote to the family
The deceased had left living up North.
"I can send the' remains when we start to have rains
And us Pine Island folks can go forth.

"So, providin' you ask it. I'll dig up the casket."
Which he did when the season brought rain.
And the river could float an old flat-bottomed boat
And the dead boy could travel again.

While moving the coffin, Bone smiled much too of'en
On the boat while en route to the car.
At the train he said, Gimme one fare from Kissimmee
To Vermont. Ain' this corpse goin' far!"

So the money was spent that the family had sent,
And a friend asked old Bone the next day:
"So you shipped the lad, hum?" Bone replied, "No, by gum –
For I thought it all over this way:

"As his kinfolks are strangers to all of us rangers,
I will give some dea Cracker this ride.
Why not make all th' fuss over some pore old cuss
Who in life hadn't wallered in pride?

"So, instead of the Yank with his money and rank
Who'd been 'round and seen lots of fun.
I jus' dug up Bill Redd and I sent him instead,
For ole Bill hadn't traveled 'round none."

At the dipping-vat, 1915

by Dale Samler, 1983
Myakka River State Park, Florida

Many a night by this old well, weary cowmen had tales to tell. . .

How storms make herds white-eyed with fright and stampede
in the dark of night;
Crossing rivers swelled high with rain - cow, man and horse
enduring pain;
Chasing bulls in scrub and slough, outwitting woods-wise
heifers, too;
A whip works best where brush is thick - both dog and horse must
know the trick
Of push and guide and push again, 'til are in the
dip-vat pen;
Those ticks near' ate the cows alive - dipped twice a month,
the cattle thrive;
Cowcatchers earn their name and pay with bone-ache work
through Saturday,
And then perhaps a night in town, where fights or rum could
knock you down;
That Cuban rum is all it's told - and Cuban wars brought
Cuban gold.

But what's to buy out in this scrub? More cows, more land,
more cowhand grub!
And where's the pleasure in this land of short return and
long demand,
Torturing 'skeeters, biting flies, an aching back and
sweat-stung eyes?
Where else on earth is one so free, becoming all that
one can be,
And learning how to be a friend, the kind that sticks,
right to the end?

. . . But most' they sat digestin' stew, pullin' on smokes
the way men do
When, day and year, the time flies fast - small time to
think of time gone past
Except, like now, when flames inspire around the cowhands'
evening fire.

A Cracker All Right

by B. Crosby Stilwell

I'm a cow-pokin' cracker
A Florida cracker - that's true
an' I don't take lightly
to nothin' I do.

I herd wild cattle
'cross flat prairie land
with a whoop an' a yell
an' a cow whip brand.

On my half-wild pony
I'm a wild-ridin' man
just making 'me a livin'
the best way I can.

Yep, a cow-drivin' cracker
who is settin' his sights
on the end of this drive
and some hell-raisin' nights.

With poker an' women
an' awhoopin' aroun'
an' a mean jug o' whiskey
up yonder in town.

'Cause I'm a cow-pokin' cracker
ain't just a po' white
but a natural-born cracker -
I'm a cracker all right.

Mrs. B. Crosby Stilwell of Madison County recorded her impressions of early Cracker cowmen. From Joe Akerman's Florida Cowman, *A History of Florida Cattle Raising*, 1976, p. 208.

CrackerFacts!

* While the name *cracker* has since taken on different meanings, its roots are found in 16th century England where the word once meant a braggart or a fast talker. In America, the term came to represent a class of rogue settlers. Whatever *cracker* may have originally implied, the term was well worn by the time cowmen began to herd their cattle through the Florida wilds in the 1800s.

Graphic by Rena Bracey, WCEU-TV Channel 15.

* References to *cracker* as a character trait appear as early as 1509, and was used in this context by William Shakespeare in King John, c. 1594: "What cracker is this same that deafes our eares with this abundance of superfluous breath?"

* The first mention of Crackers in Florida is a 1767 reference to Denys Rolle's "Crackertown" settlement on the St. Johns River near present-day Palatka. The

"Emigrant Wagon," from The Great South *by Edward King, 1875, p. 135.*

word later appears in a letter written in 1790 by Manuel de Zespedes, Governor of Spanish East Florida, who was frustrated with this lawless group of migrants.

* John Lambert's explanation in his Travels Through Lower Canada, and the United States of North America, published in 1810, is the first known reference to the term *cracker* as originating from the sound of a popping whip: "The wagoners are familiarly called crackers, from the smacking of their whip, I suppose."

* The Victorian perception of Crackers was mostly a disparaging one. In the late 19th century, Crackers were easy fodder for writers travelling through the state

looking for story ideas. The misunderstood Florida backwoods settlers were caricatured in cartoons and parodied in print across America. One of the most biting descriptions of Crackers of this period was written by George M. Barbour, a puritan New Englander who toured Florida in 1882: "The entire trip that day was through an unsettled region, the only human beings living anywhere along the road being four or five families of Florida natives, the genuine, unadulterated 'cracker' - the clay-eating, gaunt, pale, tallowy, leather-skinned sort - stupid, stolid, staring eyes, dead and lusterless; unkempt hair, generally tow-colored; and such a shiftless, slouching manner! Simply white savages - or living white mummies would, perhaps, better indicate their dead-alive looks and actions. Stupid and shiftless, yet sly and vindictive, they are a block in the pathway of civilization, settlement, and enterprise wherever they exist."

* Other writers were more sympathetic and understanding, like Samuel Fairbanks who in 1877 offered this defense of the settlers: "the Florida cracker is an independent, self-supporting citizen ... a quiet, good citizen who develops the country to some purpose by honest toil."

* Crackers were recycling long before it became popular to do so, making household items and garments out of the most unlikely of materials. Any salvaged metals were reshapened into tools, broken harnesses became belts, and cloth sacks were sewn into aprons and dresses. From Osceola County folklore is this story: "No grain is grown in these parts, and all feed ... is shipped in cotton bags. These bags are carefully saved by frugal families, bleached in the laundry and converted into all kinds of garments ... When I called on a [Cracker] woman, ... I found her wearing sackcloth made into a coarse work dress or smock, and not all the printing had been faded out, so that athwart her ample person she bore in faded pink letters the legend, 'The Perfect Form...' The 'ula' had been clipped from the last word."

* In the late 19th century, Kissimmee, Florida had America's first "ride-up" drive-through saloon, where thirsty cowhunters could buy a drink without bothering to dismount.

* To beat the mid-day summer heat, Cracker women would rise well before dawn, sometimes as early as 3 a.m., to cook bread, biscuits and meats for the rest of the day, as a hearth or a wood stove in a closed kitchen were insufferable. A hot breakfast was served at the accustomed sunrise hour, then everything

cooked that morning was placed in the middle of the table and covered by folding the corners of a table cloth over the food, which required little effort to warm up at later times of the day.

* Oxen were preferred by Crackers over mules because they were better able to

An oxen pulls a family wagon. From Harper's New Monthly Magazine, *September 1879, p. 515.*

withstand the swarms of horseflies, and because they could be eaten at the end of their service.

* Crackers traditionally eat hog jowls and blackeye peas on New Year's Eve for good luck. It's believe that the more peas you eat the more success you will have in the new year.

* Cracker cattle, still bred today, are direct descendants of Andalusian cattle introduced to Florida in 1521 by Spanish explorer Juan Ponce de Leon and British Colonial breeds from the upper South. This hardy Florida stock was bred to withstand heat, insect bites, and sparse native forage. Cracker cattle are a registered breed and are listed as one of the five most endangered domestic farm animals in America.

For More on the Florida Cracker

Akerman, Joe. A., Jr. *Florida Cowman, A History of Florida Cattle Raising.* Kissimmee, 1976.

Akerman, Joe A., Jr. "Jacob Summerlin: King of Crackers." In *Florida Pathfinders,* Lewis N. Wynne and James J. Horgan, editors. Saint Leo College Press, 1994.

Bucuvalas, Tina, Peggy A. Bulger, and Stetson Kennedy. *South Florida Folklife.* Jackson: University Press of Mississippi, 1994.

Dacy, George H. *Four Centuries of Florida Ranching.* St. Louis, 1940.

Denham, James M. "The Florida Cracker Before the Civil War as Seen Through Travelers' Accounts." *Florida Historical Quarterly* 72 (April 1994): pp. 453-462.

Denham, James M. "Cracker Woman and Their Families in Nineteenth Century Florida," In, *Florida's Heritage of Diversity: Essays in Honor of Samuel Proctor.* Mark I. Greenberg, William Warren Rogers, and Canter Brown, Jr., editors. Tallahassee: Sentry Press, 1997.

Denham, James M. *Cracker Times and Pioneer Lives, The Florida Reminiscences of George Gillett Keen and Sarah Pamela Williams,* 1998. Book forthcoming.

Edic, Robert F. *Fisherfolk of Charlotte Harbor, Florida.* Gainesville: University of Florida, 1996.

Haase, Ronald W. *Classic Cracker: Florida's Wood-Frame Vernacular Architecture.* Sarasota: Pineapple Press, Inc., 1992.

Kennedy, Stetson. *Palmetto Country.* Tallahassee: Florida A & M University Press, 1989.

Lewis, James E. "Cracker - Spanish Florida Style." *Florida Historical Quarterly* 63 (October 1984): pp. 184-204.

Matthiessen, Peter. *Killing Mister Watson.* New York: Vintage, 1991.

McWhiney, Grady. *Cracker Culture, Celtic Ways in the Old South.* Tuscaloosa and London: University of Alabama Press, 1988.

Oesterreicher, Michel. *Pioneer Family: Life on Florida's 20th Century Frontier.* Tuscaloosa: University of Alabama Press, 1996.

Pleasants, Julian M. "Frederic Remington in Florida." *Florida Historical Quarterly* 61, no. 1 (July 1977): pp. 1-12.

Rawlings, Marjorie Kinnan. *Cross Creek*. New York: Charles Scribner's Sons, 1942.

Rawlings, Marjorie Kinnan. *Cross Creek Cookery*. New York: Charles Scribner's Sons, 1942.

Smith, Patrick D. *A Land Remembered*. Sarasota, Florida: Pineapple Press, 1984.

Stein, Teresa E. *Florida Cracker Tales*. Lake Placid: Placid Publishing House, 1995.

Tebeau, Charlton W. *The Story of the Chokoloskee Bay Country with the Reminiscences of Pioneer C. S. "Ted" Smallwood*. University of Miami Press, 1955.

Tinsley, Jim Bob. *Florida Cow Hunter: The Life and Times of Bone Mizell*. Orlando: University of Central Florida Press, 1990.

Tonyan, Rick. *Guns of the Palmetto Plains, A Cracker Western*. Sarasota: Pineapple Press, Inc., 1994.

Cracker Bibliography

Akerman, Joe. A., Jr. *Florida Cowman, A History of Florida Cattle Raising*. Kissimmee: Florida Cattlemen's Association, 1976.

Akerman, Joe A., Jr. "Jacob Summerlin: King of Crackers." In *Florida Pathfinders*, Lewis N. Wynne and James J. Horgan, editors. Saint Leo College Press, 1994.

Allen, Carl. *Root Hog or Die Poor: Cracker Memories of Carl Allen*. Auburndale: Carl Allen's Cafe, 1996.

Altschul, B.J. *Cracker Cookin'*. St. Petersburg: LaFray Publishing Co., 1984.

Andrews, Allen H. *A Yank Pioneer in Florida*. Jacksonville: Douglas Printing Company, Inc., 1950.

Arnade, Charles W. "Cattle Raising in Spanish Florida, 1513 - 1763." Agricultural History 35 (No. 3), 1961. Reprinted by the St. Augustine Historical Society, Publication No. 21, 1965.

Barber, Bernice M. *From Beginnings to Boom*. Haines City, Florida: Cromer Printing, Inc., 1975.

Barbour, George M. *Florida for Tourists, Invalids, and Settlers*, 1882. Reprinted by the University of Florida Press, Gainesville, 1964.

Bartram, William. *Travels Through North & South Carolina, Georgia, East & West Florida*. Editor, Mark Van Doren. New York: Dover 1928, p. 257.

Bigelow, Gordon E., and Laura V. Monti, editors. *Selected Letters of Marjorie Kinnan Rawlings*. Gainesville: University Press of Florida, 1983.

Brown, Canter, Jr. *Florida's Peace River Frontier*. Orlando: University of Central Florida Press, 1991.

Brooks, Abbie M. *Petals Plucked From Sunny Clime*. Nashville: Southern Methodist Publishing House, 1880.

Bruce, Annette J. *Tellable Cracker Tales*. Sarasota, Florida: Pineapple Press, Inc., 1996.

Bucuvalas, Tina, Peggy A. Bulger, and Stetson Kennedy. *South Florida Folklife*. Jackson: University Press of Mississippi, 1994.

Bulger, Peggy A. "The Crackers." In *South Florida Folklife*. Tina Bucuvalas, Peggy A. Bulger, and Stetson Kennedy. Jackson: University Press of Mississippi, 1994, pp. 37 - 63.

Burke, Emily T. *Reminiscences of Georgia*. Oberlin, Ohio, 1850.

Carter, John. "Riding, Roping and Rodeoing on Heaven's Plains." *Carter Country* column, *The News-Journal*, Daytona Beach, Florida, September 27, 1986.

Cash, W.J. *The Mind of the South*. New York, 1941, pp. 72-73.

Castelnau, Comte de. "Essay on Middle Florida, 1837 - 1838," *Florida Historical Quarterly* 26, January 1948.

Claiborne, John F.H. "A Trip through the Piney Woods," *Mississippi Historical Society Publications*, 1906.

Clark, James C. "The Origin of the Florida 'Cracker'." Newspaper article in the *Florida Magazine, Orlando Sentinel* insert, July 21, 1991.

Cross, Clark I., "The Florida Cracker," in *Born of the Sun: The Official Florida Bicentennial Commemorative Book*, eds. Joan E. Gill and Beth R. Read. Hollywood, Florida: Florida Bicentennial Commemorative Journal, Inc., 1975, p. 137.

Crow, Myrtle Hilliard. *Old Tales and Trails of Florida*. St. Petersburg: Byron Kennedy and Co., 1987.

Dacy, George H. *Four Centuries of Florida Ranching*. St. Louis, 1940.

Dann, H. Carl. *Carl Dann's Vicissitudes and Casathrophics, Volume 1*. Orlando: Florida Press, Inc., 1929.

Dederer, John Morgan, "Afro-Southern and Celtic-Southern Cultural Adaptation in the Old South," paper on file, Florida State Archives.

Deland, Margaret. *Florida Days*. Boston: Little, Brown, & Company, 1889.

Denham, James M. "Some Prefer the Seminoles: Violence Among Soldiers and Settlers in the Second Seminole War,

1835 - 1842," *Florida Historical Quarterly* 70 (July 1991): pp. 38 - 54.

Denham, James M. "The Florida Cracker Before the Civil War as Seen Through Travelers' Accounts." *Florida Historical Quarterly* 72 (April 1994): pp. 453-462.

Denham, James M. "Cracker Woman and Their Families in Nineteenth Century Florida," In, *Florida's Heritage of Diversity: Essays in Honor of Samuel Proctor*. Mark I. Greenberg, William Warren Rogers, and Canter Brown, Jr., editors. Tallahassee: Sentry Press, 1997.

Denham, James M. "Cracker Times and Pioneer Lives, *The Florida Reminiscences of George Gillett Keen and Sarah Pamela Williams*." Book in preparation.

Denham, James M. *A Rogue's Paradise: Crime and Punishment in Antebellum Florida, 1821-1861* (Tuscaloosa, 1997), p. 10.

Derr, Mark. *Some Kind of Paradise: A Chronicle of Man and the Land in Florida*. New York: William Morrow and Company, 1989.

Dodd, Dorothy. "Florida in 1845: Statistics, economic life, and social life." *A Florida Historical Quarterly*, July, 1945, pp. 3-27.

Douglas, Marjory Stoneman. *Florida: The Long Frontier*. New York: Harper & Row, 1967.

Dunkling, Leslie. *A Dictionary of Epithets and Terms of Address*. London: Routledge, 1990.

Dunn, Michael. "Cracker Comeback," *The Tampa Tribune*, Saturday, May 4, 1991.

Edic, Robert F. *Fisherfolk of Charlotte Harbor, Florida*. Gainesville: University of Florida, 1996.

Elliott, Brenda J. and Joe Knetsch, Editors. *The Proceedings of the Florida Cattle Frontier Symposium*. Florida Cattlemen's Association and the Florida Cracker Cattle Breeders Association, 1995.

Fairbanks, Samuel. "The Florida Cracker," *The Semi-Tropical: A Monthly Journal Devoted To Southern Agriculture, Horticulture, and To Immigration*, September 1877, pp. 525-528.

Flexner, Stuart Berg. *Listening to America: An Illustrated History of Words and Phrases from our Lively and Splendid Past*. New York: Simon and Schuster, 1982.

Florida Department of State. *Pursuits and Pastimes: Florida Folklife in Work and Leisure*. Compiled and edited by the Florida Folklife Program, 1983.

Flynt, Wayne. *Cracker Messiah: Governor Sidney J. Catts of Florida*. Baton Rouge: Louisiana State University Press, 1977.

Fortes, Jack, "Baseball was booming a century ago." in The *Volusian*, September 22, 1996. Information courtesy of the West Volusia Historical Society.

Frisbie, Louise. *Peace River Pioneers*. Miami, 1974.

Gabbard, Alex. *Return to Thunder Road: The Story Behind the Legend*. Lenoir City, Tennessee: Gabbard Publications, 1992.

Gannon, Michael. *The New History of Florida*. Gainesville: University Press of Florida, 1996.

Garrison, Webb. *A Treasury of Florida Tales*. Nashville: Rutledge Hill Press, 1989.

Gill, Joan E. and Beth R. Read, eds. *Born of the Sun: The Official Florida Bicentennial Commemorative Book*, Hollywood, Florida: Florida Bicentennial Commemorative Journal, Inc., 1975.

Glassie, Henry. *Pattern in the Material Folk Culture of the Eastern United States*. Philadelphia: University of Pennsylvania Press, 1969.

Gramling, Lee. *Riders of the Suwannee. A Cracker Western*. Sarasota: Pineapple Press, Inc., 1993.

Gramling, Lee. *Trail From St. Augustine. A Cracker Western*. Sarasota: Pineapple Press, Inc., 1993.

Gramling, Lee. *Thunder on the St. Johns. A Cracker Western*. Sarasota: Pineapple Press, Inc., 1994.

Green, Ben. *Finest Kind: A Celebration of a Florida Fishing Village*. Macon: Mercer University Press, 1985.

Grose, Francis. *A Classical Dictionary of the Vulgar Tongue*. New York: Dorset Press, 1992, p. 102.

Haase, Ronald W. "A Personal Search for Cracker Florida," in *Florida Architect*, January/February 1987, pp. 26 - 27.

Haase, Ronald W. *Classic Cracker: Florida's Wood-Frame Vernacular Architecture*. Sarasota: Pineapple Press, Inc., 1992.

Habersham, James. "The Letters of Hon. James Habersham, 1756 - 1775" in *Collections of the Georgia Historical Society*, 15 vols. (Savannah 1904), VI.

Hall, Joseph S. *Smoky Mountain Folks and Their Lore*. Asheville: Gilbert Printing Co., 1960.

Hanna, A. J. *A Prince in their Midst: The Adventurous Life of Achille Murat on the American Frontier.* Norman: University of Oklahoma Press, 1946.

Hardy, Iza Duffus. *Oranges and Alligators: Sketches of South Florida Life.* London: Ward and Downey, 1887.

Hendrickson, Robert. *Whistlin' Dixie: A Dictionary of Southern Expressions. Volume 1, Dictionary of American Regional Expressions.* New York: Facts on File, 1993.

Henshall, James A. *Camping and Cruising in Florida*. Cincinnati: Robert Clarke & Co., 1884.

Houghton, Louise Seymour. "Ekoniah Scrub: Among Florida Lakes," *Lippincott's Magazine of Popular Literature and Science*, September 1880, pp. 265-278.

Hunter, Robert. "Looking Back," in the *Daytona Beach News-Journal* , November 3, 1996.

Johannes, Jan H. Sr. *Yesterday's Reflections - Nassau County, Florida: A Pictorial History.* Callahan, Florida: Florida Sun Printing, 1984.

Jahoda, Gloria. *The Other Florida.* New York: Charles Scribner's Sons, 1967.

Kemble, Francis Anne. *Journal of a Residence on a Georgia Plantation in 1838 - 1839* New York, 1863.

Kennedy, Stetson. *Palmetto Country*. Tallahassee: Florida A & M University Press, 1989.

King, Edward. *The Great South*, eds. W. Magruder Drake and Robert Jones. London, 1875.

Krakow, Kenneth K. *Georgia Place-Names*. Macon: Winship Press 1975.

Lamme, Louise. *Louise's Florida Cook Book: Both "Old Timey" and Modern Florida Dishes, Including Seminole Indian Recipes.* Star Publishing Company, Inc., 1968.

Lanier, Sidney. *Florida: Its Scenery, Climate and History*. Philadelphia, 1875; reprinted., Bicentennial Floridiana Facsimile Series, Gainesville: University of Florida Press, 1973.

Lewis, James E. "Cracker - Spanish Florida Style." *Florida Historical Quarterly* 63 (October 1984): pp. 184-204.

Lighter, J.E., editor. *Random House Historical Dictionary of American Slang*, Volume 1. New York: Random House, 1994.

Lyell, Sir Charles. *A Second Visit to the United States of North America*, 2 vols. New York, 1849.

Lyons, Ernest. *The Last Cracker Barrel.* New York: Newspaper Enterprise Association, Inc., 1975.

Mathews, Janet Snyder. *Edge of Wilderness: A Settlement History of Manatee River and Sarasota Bay.* Tulsa: Caprine Press, 1983.

Matthiessen, Peter. *Killing Mister Watson.* New York: Vintage, 1991.

McLeod, Michael. "Snappy Endings (Norton Baskin)," in *Florida Magazine*, September 11, 1988.

McCracken, Harold. *Frederic Remington: Artist of the Old West.* Philadelphia, 1947.

McDonald, Forrest and Grady McWhiney, "Celtic South," in *Encyclopedia of Southern Culture* , 1989.

McKay, D.B., editor. *Pioneer Florida, Volumes I and II.* Tampa: Southern Publishing Company, 1959.

McWhiney, Grady. *Cracker Culture, Celtic Ways in the Old South.* Tuscaloosa and London: University of Alabama Press, 1988.

Mickler, Ernest Matthew. *White Trash Cooking,* The Jargon Society: 10 Speed Press, 1986.

Morris, Allen. *Florida Place Names.* Sarasota: Pineapple Press, Inc., 1995.

Murat, Achille. *The United States of North America*. London, 1833.

Newell, David McCheyne. *If Nothin' Don't Happen*. New York: Alfred A. Knopf, 1975.

Oak Hill Homemakers Club. *Scrumptious Cookin'*. Oak Hill Seafood Festival, 1982.

Oesterreicher, Michel. *Pioneer Family: Life on Florida's 20th Century Frontier*. Tuscaloosa: University of Alabama Press, 1996.

O'Sullivan, Maurice, Jr., and Jack C. Lane, Editors. *The Florida Reader: Visions of Paradise from 1530 to the Present*. Sarasota: Pineapple Press, Inc., 1991.

Otto, John Solomon. Florida's Cattle-Ranching Frontier: Hillsborough County (1860). *Florida Historical Quarterly* 63, no. 1 (July 1984):pp. 71 - 89.

Owsley, Frank L. *Plain Folk in the Old South*. Baton Rouge, 1949.

Palmer, Rev. A. Smythe. *Folk Etymology: A Dictionary*. New York: Greenwood Press 1969.

Pierce, Charles W. *Pioneer Life in Southeast Florida*. Coral Gables: University of Miami Press, 1970.

Pizzo, Anthony P. *Tampa Town 1824 - 1886: The Cracker Village with a Latin Accent* . Miami: Hurricane House Publishers, Inc., 1968.

Pleasants, Julian M. "Frederic Remington in Florida." *Florida Historical Quarterly* 61, no. 1 (July 1977): pp. 1-12.

Presley, Delma E. "The Crackers of Georgia." *The Georgia Historical Quarterly* 60 (2), 1976.

Rawlings, Marjorie Kinnan. *South Moon Under*. New York: Charles Scribner's Sons, 1933.

Rawlings, Marjorie Kinnan. *Cross Creek*. New York: Charles Scribner's Sons, 1942.

Rawlings, Marjorie Kinnan. *Cross Creek Cookery*. New York: Charles Scribner's Sons, 1942.

Rawson, Hugh. *Wicked Words: A Treasury of Curses, Insults, Put-Downs, and Other Formerly Unprintable Terms from Anglo-Saxon Times to the Present*. New York: Crown Publishers, Inc., 1989.

Raymond, Paul E., letter to the editor, November 26, 1996, the *Daytona Beach News-Journal*.

Remington, Frederic. "Cracker Cowboys of Florida." *Harper's New Monthly Magazine*, XXXIX (August 1895), pp. 339 - 345.

Remington, Frederic. "Winter Shooting on the Gulf Coast of Florida." *Harper's Magazine*, XXXIX (May 1895).

Richards, Storm L. "Adaptive Features of "Cracker" Housing in North-Central Florida." *The Florida Geographer* 14, no. 2 (1980): pp. 22-25.

Robison, Jim. "Cracker cowboys earned reputation as rough riders." *The Orlando Sentinel*, September 12, 1993.

Robison, Jim. "Meager rations and hard work kept settlers going." *The Orlando Sentinel*, February 6, 1994.

Robison, Jim and Mark Andrews. *Flashbacks, The Story of Central Florida's Past*. Orlando: The Orange County Historical Society and The Orlando Sentinel, 1995.

Rogers, Benjamin F. "Florida Seen Through the Eyes of Nineteenth Century Travellers." *Florida Historical Quarterly* 34, no. 2 (October 1955).

Rouse, John E. *The Criollo: Spanish Cattle in the Americas*. Norton: University of Oklahoma Press, 1977.

Rowe, Anne E. *The Idea of Florida in the American Literary Imagination*. Gainesville: University Press of Florida, 1992.

Schafer, Daniel, "Overview of Eastern Florida Agricultural Themes, 1763-1850." Paper presented at the Northeastern Florida Plantation Symposium, Daytona Beach, March 22, 1997.

Schmidt, J. Pete. "The Painted Life of a Violent Florida Frontier." *The Floridian*, St. Petersburg Times, May 14, 1972.

Seminole Broadcasting. *The Great Florida Cattle Drive*. Video production, 1995.

Shoemyen, Janos. "Home on the Range," in *Born of the Sun: The Official Florida Bicentennial Commemorative Book*, eds. Joan E. Gill and Beth R. Read. Hollywood, Florida: Florida Bicentennial Commemorative Journal, Inc., 1975, pp. 130-132.

Smiley, Nixon. *Yesterday's Florida*. Miami: E.A. Seemann Publishing Co., 1974.

Smith, Patrick D. *A Land Remembered*. Sarasota, Florida: Pineapple Press, 1984.

Snodgrass, Mary Ellen. *An Illustrated Dictionary of Little-Known Words from Literary Classics*, Oxford: ABC-CLIO, p. 58.

Ste.Claire, Dana. "Cracker Florida: Turn-of-the-Century Backwoods Living." Florida History Notebook, *Arts & Sciences Magazine*, Fall 1991.

Ste.Claire, Dana. "Weathering Old Florida: A Historical Account of Summer Sufferance." Florida History Notebook, *Arts & Sciences Magazine*, Summer 1992.

Ste.Claire, Dana. "The Cracker in Florida Folklore." Florida History Notebook, *Arts & Sciences Magazine*, Winter 1993.

Ste.Claire, Dana. "The Cracker Mystery in Florida History." Florida History Notebook, *Arts & Sciences Magazine*, Summer 1997.

Ste.Claire, Dana and Kenneth W. Dow. "Murat: A Prince and his Palace in St. Augustine," *Florida History Notebook, Arts & Sciences Magazine,* Winter 1991.

Stein, Teresa E. *Florida Cracker Tales.* Lake Placid: Placid Publishing House, 1995.

Stringfellow, Broome. *Trek to Florida.* St. Petersburg: Great Outdoors Publishing Co., 1972.

Swift, F. R. *Florida Fancies.* New York: G. P. Putnam's Sons, 1903.

Taylor, Ann. *Tales of Florida Crackers: History, Hunting, and Humor.* Daytona Beach, Florida, 1996.

Tebeau, Charlton W. *The Story of the Chokoloskee Bay Country with the Reminiscences of Pioneer C. S. "Ted" Smallwood.* University of Miami Press, 1955.

Tebeau, Charlton W. *Florida's Last Frontier: The History of Collier County.* University of Miami Press, 1957.

Tebeau, Charlton W. *Man in the Everglades: 2000 years of Human History in the Everglades National Park.* University of Miami Press, 1968.

The Oxford English Dictionary, Second Edition. Oxford: Clarendon Press, 1989.

Thomas, Augustus. "Recollections of Frederic Remington." *Century Magazine* 86, July 1913.

Tinsley, Jim Bob. *Florida Cow Hunter: The Life and Times of Bone Mizell.* Orlando: University of Central Florida Press, 1990.

Tonyan, Rick. *Guns of the Palmetto Plains. A Cracker Western.* Sarasota: Pineapple Press, Inc., 1994.

Tonyan, Rick. "Cracking Up Cracker Myths," *Halifax Magazine*, September 1997.

Tuleja, Tad. *The New York Public Library Book of Popular Americana.* New York: MacMillan, 1994.

Valentine, Twila and Betty Chandler Williamson. *Okeechobee County: A Pictorial History.* The Donning Company, 1993.

Vann, Enoch. *Reminiscences of a Georgia-Florida Pinewoods Cracker Lawyer.* (n.p., 1937).

Washington, Ray. *Cracker Florida.* Miami: Banyan Books, 1983.

Will, Lawrence E. *Cracker History of Okeechobee.* St. Petersburg, Florida: Great Outdoors Association.

Wilson, Charles Regan, "Crackers," *Encyclopedia of Southern Culture,* Charles Regan Wilson and William Ferris, editors. Chapel Hill: The University of North Carolina Press, 1989, p. 1132.

Wynne, Lewis N. and James J. Horgan, editors. *Florida Pathfinders.* Saint Leo College Press, 1994.

Zimny, Michael. "Dog-Trots, Saddlebags, and Shotguns: Vernacular Houses in Florida." *Florida Heritage* (Spring 1996): pp. 20-23.

Index

Acknowledgments

The long and dusty trail leading to the making of *Cracker* brought me to the front porches of many colleagues, historians, journalists, Florida Crackers and others, all of whom made varied and important contributions to this work for which I am most grateful. To begin with, I cannot express enough my deepest gratitude to a very helpful Jean Hartline who volunteered her time as my "personal assistant" during the production of *Cracker*. Jean was with me throughout much of the archival and library research for this publication, and collected information for the Crackerdom self-guided tour, but most important, she kept me organized throughout the whole ordeal by ordering my office clutter. Jean, I should note, has this rare and uncanny ability to find hopelessly lost items in scattered piles of research dregs. A very special thanks to Cracker historian extraordinaire Mike Denham for many enlightening discussions, for his friendship and for his frequent words of encouragement. Mike also reviewed drafts of the first chapters of *Cracker*. Thanks, too, to Robert Austin, colleague and journal editor, for commenting on chapter drafts. Great discussions with journalist John Carter and author Rick Tonyan helped shape my perspective of Cracker life, and for this I thank them. Rich conversation with Dave and Gloria Burnell, Jim Bob and Dottie Tinsley, Robert O'Hara, Joyce Peters, Bill Dreggors, Jesse Beall, John Latham, Phil Curzio, Georgia Zern, Robert Hunter, Patrick Smith, Ron Haase, Norton Baskin, Susan Parker, Tina Bucuvalas, John Tyson, and John Willis of Custom Cracker Cookouts greatly influenced this work, as well. Timmy and Denise Kinsey of Scrambletown were very helpful in helping me reconstruct the life of Herbert Kinsey. Cracker living history specialists Reese and Jeanne Moore and Wanda Laundrie brought to life many important aspects of the Cracker way of life.

And there was ample assistance during the research phase of this publication project. Charles Tingley, Page Edwards, and Mary Herron of the St. Augustine Historical Society Library were most helpful. Charles, in particular, went far beyond the call of duty in searching out dusty, obscure works and in tolerating my "shotgun" style of research. Charles is one of Florida's finest reference librarians and his wealth of knowledge is often staggering. Joan Morris, Jody Norman, and Russell Alexander of the Florida State Archives provided much assistance in sourcing archival photographs and accessing the Stetson Kennedy files. Pamela Pape and Cindy Frederickson of the Lake Helen Public Library tracked down a number of early references for this book, and they always did it with warm smiles. The folks at the P. K. Yonge Library of Florida History at the University of Florida, Gainesville, and the University of South Florida Library took good care of me, as well. And a big thanks to James Sass of Mandala Books, Daytona Beach, one of the state's finest antiquarian book shops, for kindly allowing me to access Mandala's rich inventory - one which I would highly recommend for afternoon perusing. Lastly, Jim Bob and Dottie Tinsley were very kind to locate and loan photographs of Florida cowhunters and Bone Mizell.

The production of this book comes courtesy of a number of people. First thanks goes to Gary Libby, Director of The Museum of Arts and Sciences and the Museum's Board of Trustees for their continued support of Florida history projects and programs. Gary also served as general editor for *Cracker*. Museum book designer and friend Stacey Stivers should get a special award for her remarkable patience with me during the lengthy development and publication of this book. She is exceptional in her craft. Patricia Thalheimer, assistant editor for this work, spent a great deal of time making sure *Cracker* was in good order. Jean Hartline also provided careful proofing of the final galleys. And professional photographer and friend Roger Simms tolerated many day-long photographic forays into the backcountry of Florida, from Micanopy to Maytown. Roger would sometimes question the subject, usually an aging Cracker house or a peculiar piece of Crackerana, but would always capture its image in exacting style. The Bureau of Historical Museums, Division of Historical Resources gets a parting but huge burst of appreciation for recognizing the importance of and funding this study of the Florida Cracker culture.

Finally, my deepest appreciation goes to my wife Carol for her extraordinary patience with me and for organizing the household around my late night and weekend writing sessions, and to Casey and Saneh, two very curious and determined children, for resisting Daddy's Cracker book-writing cubbyhole . . . for hours at a time.

This publication has been financed in part with Historical Museums Grants-in-Aid Program assistance provided by the Museum of Florida History, Bureau of Historical Museums, Florida Department of State; Sandra B. Mortham, Secretary of State.
The contents and opinions of this publication, however, do not necessarily reflect the views and opinions of the Florida Department of State, nor does the mention of trade names or commercial products constitute endorsement or recommendation by the Florida Department of State.

In Memory of
Millard C. Zuber
1933-1997

One of Florida's finest Crackers

About the Author

Dana Ste.Claire is Curator of History and a professional archaeologist with The Museum of Arts and Sciences in Daytona Beach. He also directs the Old St. Augustine Village in St. Augustine for the Museum.

Born and raised in Ocala, Florida, Dana lives in the historic town of Lake Helen with his wife Carol and his two children, Casey and Saneh. He is a City Commissioner there. He attended the University of South Florida where he received a B.A. (1979) and a M.A. (1982) in anthropology. He is involved in historic preservation matters throughout Florida and currently serves as Chair of the

Casey and Dana Ste.Claire at the opening of "The Cracker Culture in Florida History" exhibition at The Museum of Arts and Sciences, June 14, 1997.

Secretary of State's Historic Preservation Advisory Council in Tallahassee.

Dana is a regular Sunday feature columnist for the Orlando Sentinel, hosts the weekly WCEU-Channel 15 television program, "Florida Crackerbarrel" on "Faces & Places," and writes for magazines and journals. His publications include two other books, *Borders of Paradise: A History of Florida Through New World Maps* with Peter A. Cowdrey (University Press of Florida), and *True Natives: Florida's First People.*